Living The High Performance Life

An Ordinary Joe's Guide to the Extraordinary

by Joe Gagnon

Managing Editors: Dana Walden and Kelly Sullivan Walden

Editor: Tom Kelsey

Copy Editor: Julie Sullivan

Cover Design: Daniella Granados

ISBN-13: 978-1979203067

Visit: www.thehighperformancelife.net

DEDICATION

My dream is that everyone who chooses to live their own version of a high performance life gets the immense amount of support that I got from my family and friends. Thank you to my wife Anthea and daughters, Julianne and Kimberly. You believed in me at such a level that I was able to do more than I thought I could.

ACKNOWLEDGMENTS

Taking a lifetime of experiences, thousands of blog posts and a lot of big ideas and turning it into a book requires help and partnership from many who believed in this project and the message that it carries. Dana Walden, Kelly Sullivan Walden, Tom Kelsey, Anca Van Assendelft, thank you very much.

TABLE OF CONTENTS

Author's Note:

It seems improbable to me that the diversity of people I meet around the world all have the same initial reaction to "Living The High Performance Life" (aka THPL). They will say things like:

> *I can never do what you have done.*
> *I can't run.*
> *I am not a CEO.*
> *I am too busy.*

…. and the list goes on and on…

So, maybe an explanation is required.

Let's start with the fact that I'm an average guy. I have no special "DNA", and not only was I not a high school track star, it never occurred to me that I could even run (except to avoid the bullies). My dad was a social worker in the NYC schools and my mom, when she was not taking care of me and my siblings and I, worked as a teacher. My version of high performance back then was playing on the swing set in the backyard for extended periods of time.

It took a long while before I realized that a key ingredient to success was - being willing to do more than the next guy. In other words, the gap between being successful— or not— was in doing more than I thought I could. But this experiment did not immediately produce results. There were setbacks and challenges, modest jobs, modest experiences, and some outright failures along the way. My dreams were always big but the path to achieve them was not all that obvious.

Sound familiar? Yea, I am just like you.

We have a nice life and yet we know there is more out there. But, how do we get at it?

That is the question.

I've written the book I wish I had back then when I was looking for ideas, support, guidance, coaching, anything that could've helped me. Back then when I was not flush with a network of connected people, a resource like my THPL book—with the techniques, stories, exercises and examples— would have been an amazing asset. What I needed was a handbook for life of sorts, one that I could use whenever I needed a boost, guidance, or out-of-the-box ideas.

I don't know where I'd be now if I'd had access to a resource like this—one that seemed like only "those" other people had. I wonder what my life would have been like if I had my own copy of "Living the High Performance Life" back then. I imagine it would have given me a clue about what to do about those big dreams and plans. With a book like this, it definitely wouldn't have taken me so long to figure it out.

This is how this book came together: I started to reflect and to look back, on my life successes and failures, so that I could pull out the "nuggets" the "gems" that blossomed as I lived my version of THPL. I started writing them down in my daily blog over five years ago. I started off using myself as a Guinea Pig…and using my blog as a reminder for how to think and how to apply the THPL principles to my everyday life.

I really like the handbook approach. It is not that we all need to do all of what is in the book. No way! Rather, before you start reading, begin this process simply. Start with something you can control – your mindset. Success breeds success. If you start with a way of thinking that sets you up to do just a little bit more than you think you can, then you've effectively set yourself up for success!

Allow me to emphasize, **you do not need to adopt all practices and techniques of THPL** to start to live a life that aligns you with a better version of yourself. And, you do not have to dedicate 100% of your time to living at the highest level – rather what you can do, is simply embrace what THPL stands for and then use as much or as little as you want to give you a consistent boost.

You can put in more time and effort one year and then less another year. The key is to be purposeful about how you go about living your life, from this moment forward. If you are too busy – then only use part of the book, and when you want more, do more. This book is designed to be your handbook for life, a resource you use when you want to be inspired, when you need some advice, when you want to try something new, and when you want to do more and be more than you thought you could.

By reading this now, you are already well on your way! And remember this book is not about running...it is about finding your own unique talent and mission and doing more than you think you can on your own personal journey. A better teacher, artist, salesperson, golfer, McDonald's manager, stay-at- home mom...whoever and whatever and wherever you are The High Performance Life can apply to you.

PART I –
INTRODUCTION

OK…Let's get this out of the way FIRST

In this world of motivational speakers, fitness gurus, spiritual leaders, get-whatever-it-is-you-want-now fads… how do you sort through the glut of approaches that are served up by those who seem to personify nothing but superlatives in their appearance, attitudes and actions? In other words, why should you believe that what I have to say is in any way better than the rest? It is a fair question.

What I can tell you is the stories and practices I share with you here are drawn from my own personal experience, a journey of a lifetime, not fleeting or temporal. While I have led a life that has been somewhat extraordinary by some measures, I was not born with a silver spoon in my mouth, nor with much more than average physical or mental talents.

None of us sets out to be remarkable. Our lives are just "our lives." The "spin" is that the conscious choices we make allow us to create a more remarkable version of that life. I will share with you how I've done that but I also know that if you can…

Live in the Mystery...
Show up,
Believe in the Process,
And let go of your Expectations...
...Magic becomes real,
And Dreams come true,
As Power, Passion and Possibility conspire to unleash your
version of
The High Performance Life.

Warning: This book may push your buttons.

Overview

"The most special thing about me is that I am an average man." – **Buckminster Fuller**

I'm an ordinary Joe. I wasn't born with any particular advantage or stand-out gifts. In fact, growing up, I had a few things going against me. Physically speaking, I was:

1. The shortest
2. The skinniest
3. The smallest of my classmates

I was the one boy in the Catholic grammar school class picture who had to line up in the front row *with the girls (ewwww)*, and the very last of the boys to have their voice change from a high falsetto to anything resembling a baritone. Even now, as hard as I try, I'll never give Barry White a run for his money. In other words, I was the kind of "wimpy kid" the bullies loved to experiment on with their new-found intimidation tactics.

Looking back, it's a miracle I survived growing up in the rough and tumble neighborhoods of New York. In fact, it was all I could do to hide in the shadows so as to not be picked on by all the other guys my age, who weren't just shaving, by the way. No, the guys in my neighborhood by the time they were in high school had nests of curly hair protruding from their muscled chests, showcasing their gold chains, glinting in the afternoon sun, as they drove by in their Monte Carlos, with giggling girls hanging on their arms. You get the idea? Growing up, it was not fun being me. And that's just how it was.

But, like a tree that grows in Brooklyn, in spite of the fact that my early years were beyond challenging, because of the principles and practices I discovered along the way (by the grace of God), I now have a life that, honestly, is so remarkable, sometimes I have to pinch myself.

Among the things that most blow my mind, is the fact that I've been married for 30 years to a most supportive wife who allowed me to be me and I have two phenomenal daughters in whom I am incredibly proud; I've been a

University president, CEO of several successful companies, I speak on stage inspiring thousands of people around the world; I travel more than anyone I know (over four million air miles, more than 5,000 nights in hotels; I've visited all 50 United States—twice over, and explored more than 40 different countries. And since I started jogging at the ripe old age of 40 (beginning with struggling to complete one mile), I've since then logged over 30,000 miles running and 100,000 biking, completed six Ironman triathlons, 15 ultra-marathons, and 34 marathons, and most recently, I completed a "6-Continent Challenge" (a marathon a day, for 6 days on 6 continents). If there is a "What's Next?" t-shirt, I have definitely earned it!

If you get nothing else from my book (and I hope you get a LOT more than this), I hope you'll be emboldened with the knowledge that even if your life doesn't look the way you want it to, if you've ever been bullied by boys in Monte Carlos, ever felt like you didn't fit in, or you haven't yet come into a life that you love, know that it's not only possible for you to have a remarkable life (a High Performance Life), it's your destiny...if you do your part of the equation.

Your part of the equation is what this book is all about.

There's a saying, "To the one whom much has been given, much is expected." I've been given the same amount as everyone else, as the subtitle of this book suggests, I'm an ordinary Joe. But, because of certain decisions I've made, and practices I've created along the way, I've turned my life's path into a journey that many people have told me inspires them. It is now my passion, privilege, and honor to share with you what I've learned. So, if you're like me and are ready to live a life you create, instead of the default life that was handed to you, The High Performance Life (or THPL for short) can lead you to your own personal fulfillment beyond your wildest dreams.

Allow me to demystify it for you:

THPL JOURNEY

LIFE (SOUL)

With positive emotions and a no-constraint mindset, we make well-balanced choices, and take well-guided actions, surrounded by a loving and supportive community.

LEARNING (MIND)

Seeking information and knowledge that enables us to improve our behaviors, increase competencies, and achieve a maximum state of readiness.

FITNESS (BODY)

Integrating physical and spiritual activity, combined with nutrition, into our daily lives, to create a **mind/body/soul** connection that is both **healthy and powerful**.

A Healthy, Capable, Present and Powerful Mind, Body & Soul

Trends Are Easy to Spot (in the rearview mirror)

It's fascinating to look back and analyze why you are who you are. Everything that's happened, the people you've met, by chance or by design, every second of it has delivered you to this very moment, right now (and all those that follow). Still, there are those moments in our lives we'd rather forget.

Maybe you smashed up your dad's car, flunked a test, or let a friend down. At the moment of disappointment, you have two choices:

OPTION 1: You can run and hide, or find someone else to blame.

~ OR ~

OPTION 2: You can stand up and say,
"Yes, I did that, and I'm responsible for my actions.
I won't do it again."

I've learned from experience that Option 1 doesn't work. It just creates more problems. On the other hand, the liberation that comes from Option 2 is very empowering.

At the same time, it can be a challenge, because we have an inherent desire to be "perfect", whether or not we can admit it. The truth is, we should have no expectation of perfection, and it is a fool's game to pursue it. What we can expect is agency over our own behavior and the choices we make at key moments. It's at these turning points that we will find out what we are made of.

One of the most important choices I've learned to make is to grab hold of the tough life lessons and own them. This has now become a habit of mine, and a rewarding one for sure.

In Other Words…

Take responsibility for your part.

Forgive yourself.

Make a plan about how you will do it differently next time. And experience the exhilaration as it propels you forward.

Oh yes, *now* watch the rearview mirror, as your problems become indistinguishable dots in your past.

CHAPTER 1 –
Words That Trigger Me

There are a few words and phrases that trigger me. When I hear these words, I am bothered. Bothered because we can do something about them. And if we can't do anything about it, *why* not? What's getting in the way? I have made it my life's work to recognize this and do something about it.

Here's my first "trigger word":

Disappointment

It affects me very deeply if someone tells me I've disappointed them. When my inability to execute to the best of my abilities has let someone else down, I view it as a personal failure. If I have disappointed you or anyone else, I have no one to blame but myself. It's all on me.

And I'm not content to end with blame, because that's not the point. Today, I react to my "disappointment trigger" by saying, "Wow, how would I do that differently if given another opportunity?" Once I figure out how I could improve the situation, I commit to making it right…one way or another.

Which leads me to Trigger Word #2:

Excuse

I've written my own definition of excuse (no offense, Mr. Webster). In my definition, an "excuse" is simply the inability to take responsibility for one's actions.

If you've ever played golf and hit the ball into the woods, have you ever felt the impulse to blame everything else: the wind, someone talking, an annoying fly, a painful childhood memory? When perhaps you should consider the fact that you looked up, rolled your wrist, or didn't properly transfer your weight?

You hit the ball into the woods. What's the big problem? Go find it and do your best to not hit it into the woods again.

This isn't just a sports analogy. You can "miss" in anything you do, especially those occasions where you put a lot on the line. So what if you make a mistake and miss the mark?

No Big Deal.

Figure out what you did wrong, then do what you can to avoid it in the future. And if you find yourself making the same mistake more than once, hire a coach or ask for help to figure out how to put an end to that.

It's that simple. Take accountability and responsibility for your actions, no matter what you've done. Only good things will come from this.

Trigger Words #3 and #4

My feathers also get ruffled when I hear any form of *"It's impossible,"* or *"You can't do that."* When I think back through my life and everything I have ever achieved, I realize it all came from a personal decision to do something, quite often exactly the thing that others told me was impossible to do.

I did it anyway.
I didn't try to do it.
I just did it.

Everyone on this planet has a similar opportunity to achieve personal goals, far beyond their own wildest dreams. If we are truly earnest and ask that pivotal question: *Why <u>not</u> go for it?* It becomes more challenging to come up with reasons to do nothing.

I believe that when you put anything resembling an excuse in the way of your dream or goal, by definition, you are choosing a life of disappointment, one that is far less than it could be. Why would you want that? Especially when a better world is there for you, if you just reach out and live it.

Since you are reading this book I assume you are human … and since you are human, I can tell you unequivocally that *your personal potential is off the charts!*

One of my biggest passions and reasons for writing this book is to offer you the opportunity to commit to a life with no more excuses, so that together we can explore and embrace all that is humanly possible.

CHAPTER 2 –
Middle School/
Minnie Mouse

I've always been on the "small side." I was the one boy in the Catholic grammar school class picture who had to line up in the front row with the girls, so looking back at those class photos always makes me cringe. I didn't come into my adult height until after High School, so as you might imagine, I did not hang out among the jocks. They had a name for kids like me:

The 2:35 Club

You knew the kids in the 2:35 Club because when the school bell rang at the end of the day, we all just disappeared. We weren't on any of the teams or in any of the clubs.

My family also wasn't in the "in-crowd." We were conservative, church-going Catholics who rarely socialized. Family mattered most. My father was a social worker who devoted his life to helping troubled adolescents in some of the harshest neighborhoods of New York City, so he routinely dealt with a level of challenge many of us can barely comprehend. It made him, and my mother, tremendous role models, something I've tried to emulate throughout my life.

And let me tell you, as I mentioned earlier, it wasn't easy growing up as a small, skinny, teenager in Yonkers, New York, with a high-pitched voice, and hating to answer the phone for fear of hearing,

"Hello miss, may I speak to your Mother or Father?"

Those awkward teen years made me truly appreciate the meaning of unconditional love...because my self-esteem needed all the help it could get.

Before you start feeling sorry for me, here's a spoiler alert:

Things eventually did work out for me (in spades, I might add).
But as is often the case, they got worse before they get better.

Meet Minnie Mouse

The Golden Arches, Big Mac, Fries and a large Coke. You can almost taste it, right? For me it was my first job, starting as the lowest guy on McDonalds' totem pole. Regardless of my lowly stature, I was overjoyed, proud to have a job and to earn some money and feel like a real success.

If you've never had the dubious privilege of working in the fast-food industry, you will know that *no one* is overjoyed about being there. Because my co-workers were always ticked off, they took their frustration out on me in a never-ending stream of jabs, both overt and subtle.

So here I am. The skinny late bloomer with the high-pitched voice, and what did this whole package remind my co-workers of? A mouse. And not just any mouse. Not even Mickey Mouse, which would have been fine by me. *Minnie Mouse*. The girl mouse! That's what they called me.

Just what I needed. Another nail in the coffin of my self-confidence.

None of them ever knew how much their attacks devastated me. I never let on how terribly their cruel words made me feel, or how many times I hid in the storeroom to cry.

I fantasized about fighting back with all the witty comebacks I would make, but something inside me told me that if I engaged, I would be tangling in their same hateful energy. What good would that do?

I learned from my Dad that bullies act from their own insecurity and weakness. With this awareness, I resolved that I wouldn't let them weaken me or bring me down to their level. Instead of rage, I gave them silence. Regardless of the emotions boiling up inside me, I never once let them have the pleasure of knowing it bothered me. If I gave them legitimacy, the "outsiders" would be in charge. If I chose *not* to be the victim, I was running the show.

Right there, at the tender age of 17, I realized that the real fight wasn't coming from outside. It was coming from inside me. I turned "Minnie Mouse" from a weakness into fuel for my personal strength; my inner *"Mighty Mouse, [1]"* as the case may be.

The point here isn't to become a control-freak sociopath who disregards valid input from others. The point is to be able to decide what, and who, to believe. Because I didn't listen to my tormentors or give them the kind of feedback that made the game fun for them, they eventually got bored and stopped.

If I could only pass this knowledge on to every victim of bullying in the world, I would feel that my life has been worthwhile.

I worked two full years at McDonalds, and only quit when I had already identified my next job and was ready to move on. And today, in spite of the fact that I still sometimes

---

[1] Apologies to anyone born after 1965

shudder when I drive by those golden arches (and I honestly *never* eat there), I thank Ray Kroc *and* the late great Walt Disney for their part laying the groundwork of The High Performance Life journey that is now as much a part of my day as breathing.

CHAPTER 3 –

I Am My Career

1995. I was 35 years old, working 100 hours a week, on the fast track at Ernst & Young, then one of the "Big Six" accounting firms that dominated the industry. Sleep was for sissies. Who needed a vacation? My goals were clear: to be one of the youngest to make partner by doing it before my 36th birthday. How?

Say yes to everything.

Never stop.

Never slow down.

I will admit, there was a palpable energy, an emotional high, as I directed big projects and ordered dinner-in because we were pulling yet another all-nighter. And when the work was done, we all went out together and played. Hard. We didn't have lives of our own, and if we did, we largely ignored them.

There were many moments of significance during my E&Y career that afforded me choices, many of which set a foundation for future strength and built resiliency into my life. One of particular note happened while I was at our annual Customer Tech Conference in Tucson, Arizona. On top of my regular client work, I volunteered to chair the event and show the partners that I could do it all (LOL).

And it worked! Fueled with caffeine, hotel pastries and adrenalin, we pulled the whole thing off without a hitch: *big* kudos from the big suits. Now it was time for us to go out and celebrate our conquest.

The beer flowed, and in a very short time created that perfect opposition between IQ and testosterone, setting the stage for a true "Mano y Mano[2]" event: arm wrestling! At first I just watched, feeling no need to involve myself. Match after match, it got more interesting. More beer. Less brains.

Off to the side stood another guy, who I'll call Gary. He was almost as disinterested as me, but he caught my eye and I thought, "Why not?" Gary didn't look like much of an opponent. He was a real "type B" guy with a slight build, who could easily dissolve into the wallpaper, or so I thought.

---

[2] There is a popular misconception that "Mano y Mano" translates as "man to man." It literally means "hand in hand."

Before I knew it, my alcohol/testosterone party was ready to roll, and there I was sitting across the table from Gary, excited to arm wrestle him. As we clenched fists, I tried intimidating him with a stare, but he wouldn't even look me in the eye. This guy was going to be a breeze!

It took him about seven seconds to pin me.

In stunned amazement, I demanded a rematch, thinking,

"Okay Joe, you've gotta <u>beat</u> this guy!"

This time, he did look me in the eye, before taking about five seconds to pin me again. I was incredulous! Since my "Minnie Mouse" days I thought I had taken physical fitness seriously and, while I prided myself in being able to do pushups and pullups and sit-ups, I realized at that moment that I had lost both my rhythm, and my strength.

And I had just lost to Gary.

Twice.

So what did I do? I made excuses, of course!

Forget it! It's just arm wrestling!
No time to work out because I was working so hard on
getting ahead on the job.
There are much more important things to worry about.

But I just lost! To Gary! Twice!

And then, for reasons I don't wholly understand, a surge of terror rattled me to my core.

Was this the body I was going to inhabit the rest of my life?!

I saw a crystal clear fork in the road ahead. If I continued down the current path I was on I might appear strong, but beneath the surface I would always be weak and insufficient, playing to some middle-of-the-road future. I looked ahead on that road and saw an endless rut that just continued to deepen.

Or I could take a new path of *power, passion* and *possibility* from this moment forward. To reach higher, and find out what "more" would be like, though not in the form that we typically expect (money, professional power, acquisition). More of the power and passion that I now believed could only come from within. More as in the dawning of a belief that I could be more, and do much more than I had ever given myself permission to think was possible. I'll be honest, I had no idea where this new path would lead me, just a profound feeling that it was the right thing to do.

I took another lesson away from my arm-wrestling match with Gary: If I was going to lose at something, it would never again be for lack of trying, or lack of readiness. If I lost, despite my best efforts, if I couldn't turn it into an inspirational event, I would at least make it informative rather than demoralizing.

Any failure I experienced would only make me smarter, stronger, and more resilient. From that moment on, I began a living experiment, to see what I am capable of, to test the limits of what we are all capable of, which has now expressed itself as The High Performance Life. And I've made fitness one of the core priorities in my life.

It began with three days a week of exercise, then four, five, and now it's a daily ritual; as much a part of my life as brushing my teeth, eating and sleeping. As of this writing, I've completed more than 34 marathons, six Ironman Triathlons and fifteen Ultra-Marathons, hundreds of thousands of pushups and pullups, and a total of more than 130,000 training miles (and counting). And I've got the log books to prove it, because I've tracked every day of my training since that eye-opening night when Gary pinned me. And it all came together in April of 2017, when I completed a task that I have been dreaming about for several years. I ran six marathons, on six *separate continents*, on six *consecutive days*, something we named "Run Joe Run." You can read more about this in the last chapter of the book.

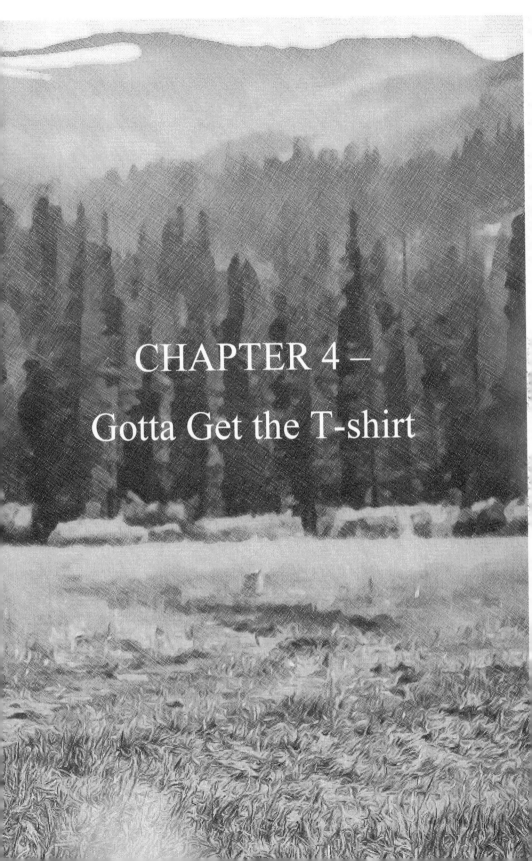

CHAPTER 4 –

Gotta Get the T-shirt

Important Note: **In the spirit of full disclosure, I'm now about to tell you one of the craziest things I've ever done. The first time I told this story, I was the CEO of a company that was in dire straits, when throwing in the towel would have seemed like an easy, even <u>practical</u>, thing to do.**

I'll warn you, this story might push some buttons. And while it will definitely help you know me a lot better, how it affects you might help you know yourself better, too. Here goes.

As a veteran of endurance sports, I've faced numerous occasions when *quitting* seemed like an obvious choice. Endurance sports includes 26.2 mile Marathons, Century (100 mile) bike rides, Triathlons (combined swimming/biking/running) Ultra-Marathons (anything over 26.2 miles/up to over 100 miles), and then the big-daddy of them all: The Ironman.

Created as the ultimate test of endurance athletics, the Ironman stands out as a particularly grueling affair: a 2.4 mile swim, followed by a 112 mile bike ride, and then a 26.2 mile marathon.

The crazy people who compete in these events don't do it for money or fame. In fact, the only tangible reward you get, unless you are one of the top finishers is an event-themed silkscreened "finisher" T-Shirt, retail value about $20.

The *intangible* reward is that you get to hear the greatest words any endurance athlete can hear when you cross the finish line: "(YOUR NAME HERE), you are an Ironman.[3]"

---

[3] Of course, the flip side is a "DNF.," which means "Did Not Finish." This can happen for a number of reasons: weather, mishaps, or equipment failures, to name a few. Then there are competitors who just aren't fully prepared for these ultimate endurance tests. It's clearly not for everyone. Regardless of the reason, "DNF" is the last thing any racer wants next to his or her name on the final results.

November 2010 – The Panama City, Florida Ironman

This was my second Ironman, and I was determined to beat my time from the previous race, so I trained for an entire year, fourteen workouts a week. Swim. Bike. Run. Swim. Bike. Run, consuming 4,000 calories a day, pushing as hard as my body would allow in a calculated regimen, engineered to deliver me to full readiness by race day.

As race day approached, I planned a tapering period so that I would arrive at the starting line perfectly prepared to attack the course.

The race day was Saturday, but I came in the preceding Thursday to get acclimated to the locale and feed off the intoxicating vibe as thousands of other competitors streamed in. I took care of my registration and technical chores and had an easy couple of days. I never completely stopped training, but by Friday all that was left was a five-mile ride and a one mile run, almost an afterthought at that point.

Keeping with a tradition of mine, I had a big ice cream the night before the race, first because I love it, but more importantly, because it provided me with yet another dose of calories that my body would be craving by the following afternoon.

At 3:30 AM the alarm rang and a familiar, anxious, excitement bubbled up inside me. The race wouldn't start until 7:00 am, but it was important to eat a good breakfast, get my personal hygiene out of the way, pull on my wet suit and head on over to the starting line.

Despite the fact that we were in Florida, the morning was cold and dark, so I stayed warm by breathing deeply and capturing as much body heat as I could from the crowd of three thousand others in wet suits and swim caps surrounding me. Aside from the soft sound of the waves, an eerie silence set in.

The only talking going on was inside our minds. People were thinking everything from, "Let's just get to it" to "Let me come to my senses and run from here." I'm thinking

"It's all good. I've trained perfectly. I've eaten. I'm *ready* for this."

As the pre-race ceremonies commenced, during the playing of the National Anthem I felt a rush of emotions. I'm not sure whether it was my patriotic upbringing or an intense sugar overdose, but, an enormous sense of hope for all of humanity overwhelmed me. By the time we got to "and the home of the brave." I was ready to start bawling.

I snapped out of it as the PA announcer began the final countdown and a huge cheer spontaneously swelled in the surrounding crowd.

10-9-8-7-6-5-And-The-Gun-Goes-BANG!

I sprinted down the sand and hit the cool Gulf waters head first.

The rising sun just crossing the horizon lit up the thousands of swimmers surrounding me in an amber glow against the sparkling waves. Then it was just one stroke after another. Stroke. Breathe. Stroke. Breathe. All-Is-Well. Stroke-And-Breathe.

I was relaxed, looking around, amazed at the incredible spectacle I was a part of. Before I knew it, I was charging out of the water with a personal best swim time! Amazing!

I peeled off my wetsuit, and put on my biking shorts and bike shirt which I would wear for the rest of the day. I prefer that to a running shirt, because it has handy pockets in back to store your stuff, like arm warmers and gloves, food and sun glasses, should I need them.

I pulled on my socks and cinched my biking shoes as fast as I could and then hopped on my bike with unbridled enthusiasm for the day ahead. Everything went great, right through the 89th mile of the ride. Then boom! I went over the handlebars. How this occurred I will never know, but over I went and out went the lights.

As I came back to consciousness all I recall was a group of faint voices saying "Don't move! Stay still!" "Who are they warning?" I wondered. Then I gradually realized they were talking to *me*.

Woozy, bleeding, in a lot of pain, I did what any good racer would do. I got up and picked up my bike to get back on. I could vaguely hear them yelling at me to lie back down, and that an ambulance would arrive shortly. But an overriding power in my head kept saying,

"Gotta get the t-shirt."

The $20 "finisher's shirt," sitting there folded up on the table, just waiting for me to come get it.

Under the distant and frantic pleas of the Good Samaritans, and before that ambulance could arrive, I did my best to adjust my bike back into something I could ride. And in the midst of the commotion I slipped through the crowd, climbed aboard my battered bike and pedaled off, with "Gotta-get-the-t-shirt" now a pulsing mantra.

Do I sound crazy yet? Wait. It gets better.

The first thing I realized was I couldn't shift. The derailleur was broken and so instead of 20 speeds, I had *one*. It was stuck in the lowest gear, so I would need to pedal extra hard to go anywhere. And my new top speed would be about 10 mph. This, after I'd been going north of 22 mph to this point.

Like a turtle in quicksand, I pedaled onward, now keenly aware of several other things.

First I still had 21 miles to ride on this wobbly single-speed bike. And after that would come the 26.2 mile Marathon leg. Next, my knee and ribs were starting to hurt. A lot[4]. And last, most of the racers I had outpaced thus far were now streaming past me in large numbers.

Up and over the causeway, a 100-foot arch I now had to climb. Slower. Slower. I barely made it to the top. Next

---

[4] I later found out the pain was due to two broken ribs and a fractured right kneecap, along with assorted contusions and a concussion.

was Beach Road with a huge headwind swirling around the condos, buffeting me as I pedaled onward.

It was 80 degrees and I was shivering. "Why am I cold?" I wondered. I would later learn that was because shock was setting in.

I pulled on my arm warmers and gloves. More people passed me by. "Gotta-get-the-t-shirt" pounding inside my head.

As I pedaled on, I started focusing on Plan "B," now that Plan "A" was toast. If I could get to the transition, maybe I could walk the marathon and still make it before the cut-off? The official cut-off time was 17 hours. I did some mental math and calculated that it was possible!

Finally, I made it to the transition point between bike and run, and the voices in my head started chattering once more. This would be a perfect time to call it a day. All of my stuff was there. No one would notice. I did have a good workout, 2.4 miles in the water, 112 miles on the bike. Almost anyone would call that a great day's work. I could hang out and relax, right?

The committee between my ears kept debating these points as I gingerly stepped off my bike and limped into the transition tent, doing my best to avoid the concerned stares of officials and onlookers.

Then that powerful voice came back on top of the rest, with that steady "Gotta get the t-shirt" mantra, over and over again.

I decided right there that quitting was not an option. I got to this point and if I could keep moving then I would keep moving.

How about now? Do I sound crazy enough?

I picked up my transition clothing bag and set out to put on my running shoes. Ooops. Easier said than done, as the searing pain in my ribs made it almost impossible to bend over far enough to pull my running shoes on.

After struggling in vain for some time, a kindly volunteer came over and helped get my running shoes on. After only 18 minutes[5] in the transition, I was ready to go.

Those first few steps were brutal, and the cheering fans didn't help me feel any better. They were just a reminder of how slow I was going and how much I hurt. And while the warm temperatures should have made me feel good, I still couldn't stop shivering.

At mile four, an aid station "angel" with Advil, potato chips, and coke provided a moment of respite and the energy boost I needed to plod on. I remember a feeling of hope glimmering as I noticed fewer people were passing me. Of course, that's because I was falling still further toward the back of the pack.

This leg of the race (pun intended) was hard enough without the beating my ego was taking, as throngs of onlookers now got to witness the pathetic spectacle of me

---

[5] Usually the transition takes about 2-3 minutes to complete.

limping along like an old man. And because my name and number were plastered on the front of my shirt, they all chanted "Go Joe, go!"

Normally I would love hearing this, but today I just wanted to disappear. I didn't feel one bit heroic. I wanted to yell at them, "I don't normally shuffle along like this! I'm usually a really good runner!" But I didn't say a word aloud. Instead, my "Gotta get the T-Shirt" power-voice was now in a screaming match with the ones telling me to stop this madness.

Sunset at Mile 20. 6.2 miles to go. Didn't think I could get any colder. I got colder.

I now arrived at the darkest moment I pray I will ever have in my life. Stop or finish? The battle was on, deep in my soul, each mile testing my worth.

Mile 21, 22, 23. Gotta…get…the…t…shirt.

Now the mile signs were missing. "Where am I?" How would I know where the end was?! All I knew was that if I stopped I would collapse.

Am I crazy enough yet?

Absolutely!

Quit? Nope!

Gotta Get The T-Shirt!

Mind and body began to spiral downward. Where's the bottom? One more turn. And then, finally something I recognized.

The finish line!

I shuffled down the final corridor between the two columns of fan-filled bleachers, signs and décor. The crowd was still there cheering on anyone who had made it to this point. For it is only the really crazy ones who cross the finish line in an Ironman race. And today, for sure, I qualified on a singular new dimension of nuts.

At that moment , I very much appreciated the cheers as these diehard supporters hooting up a storm for the "dead man running." And at last, after almost 12 hours 45 minutes[6] I heard those cherished words, like music to my ears: "Joe Gagnon, you are an Ironman."

I never get tired of hearing that.

I stumbled across the line and fell into the arms of two stunned volunteers.

"Are you okay?" they probed with concerned urgency.

"Now that I'm done, yes." Is all I could answer!

They loaded me into a wheelchair to be whisked into the medical tent where I would soon discover just how messed up I really was. But not before I forced them to let me stand up for the finisher picture, which shows me smiling as I heard my inner voice say,

"I got the T-Shirt."

---

[6] World record Iron Man times are about 5 hours faster than this.

I also discovered that I had a concussion, two broken ribs and a fracture in my right kneecap, along with assorted contusions. I'll admit, it took more than a few weeks to recover, but today I'm as good as new.

My helmet saved my life that day and I will never get on a bike without one, no matter what the distance or the speed. It served its purpose. With all of the earnestness I can summon, I beg you to do likewise. There are those who have told me that was flat-out the dumbest thing I have ever done. There are a few who are amazed at my tenacity, and a few more who are horrified by it.

For me it was none of the above. It was a life-changing moment, in which I discovered myself, precisely where I was, at precisely the moment I was in.

The impossible became the possible.
A switch was thrown in my mind that changed my outlook, and my ability to handle whatever comes my way, with the following realization:

Pain is temporary.
Quitting is <u>forever</u>.

If I had given up, my experience of that race would have ended before the ambulance ever got there, and that would be it. DNF. No other possible outcome. How much more final can it get? Think about that, the next time you're facing a challenge that might cause you a bit of discomfort or even pain. The pain will, most probably, go away. Quitting never does.

And as I look back at this whole event, beside the fact that I have promised myself, my family, and many others that I will never, ever, repeat something like that again, I can't help but make the even greater realization.

We can do much more than we think we can.

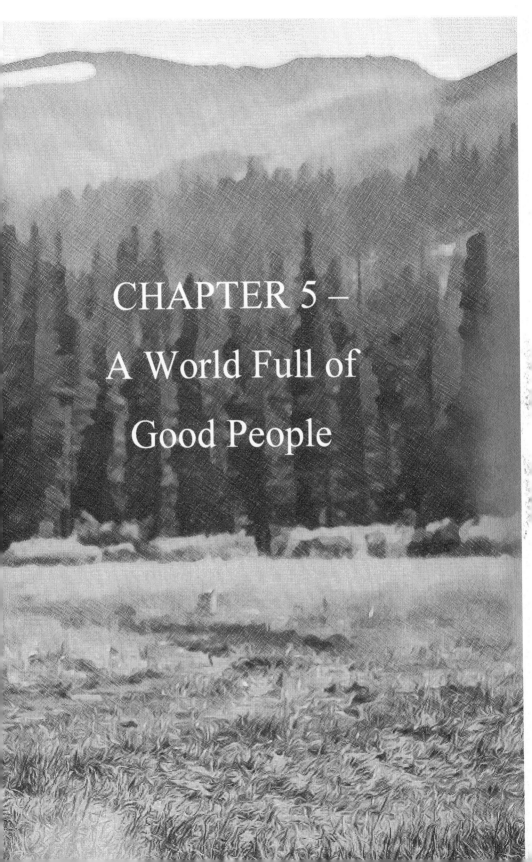

CHAPTER 5 –
A World Full of
Good People

You've now heard several episodes from my life that help illustrate who I am, and how I've come to these beliefs that I hold dear. I will, from time to time, dip back into personal experience to illustrate or amplify something, but let me summarize by saying that I've now held numerous positions in 12 different companies, from the lowest guy at McDonalds, to Partner at one of the biggest accounting and consulting firms in the world, to CEO of a major software company.

I have traveled to every state in the US, and to every corner of our world, and I want you to know that, in spite of what you read in the news or watch on TV, my personal experience tells me:

The world is full of really good people,
AND I am one of them, just as I know you are, too.

I don't want to just be a good person. I want to be *great*. And not great like Babe Ruth or Caesar Augustus. Great as in the *best possible version of me that I can be*.

This shows itself as burning desire and an ever-growing belief that we all have tremendous power inside of us.

When we tap into our true selves,
And reach down deep to pull out all that's possible,
We are capable of creating a life of magic.

When we know this about ourselves and experience it firsthand, it helps to expand the way we see life and our place in it. We move past merely surviving to a much greater state of being. And you can call me greedy, but I want to do more than just survive. I want to thrive.

Let me break it down to the simplest terms:

Life
Learning
Fitness

Just as water is synthesized by combining one oxygen and two hydrogen atoms, these three essential elements combine to become The High Performance Life. Obviously, "life" is first, but this means much more to me than just a regular heartbeat and strong metabolism. I'm talking about "Life", with a capital "L," the precious gift we all share.

We come hardwired with the understanding that we owe it to whoever bestowed this gift upon us to do everything in our power to make it the best we can. Not just a good life, a giving life, an abundant life.

A High Performance Life

Living The High Performance Life doesn't mean you are competing with anyone else. But if and when you do compete, you will be doing so at the highest level you can.

You will be the best possible "you" that you can be.

And if you don't win, you *learn*, so you always win!

That is why *lifelong Learning* is the second pillar of THPL. Absorbing all you can from each and every encounter, whether it's reading a blog or book, watching a YouTube video, discussing with a friend or coworker, mopping the floors at McDonalds, or flipping over the handlebars of a bike.

When you're living The High Performance Life, learning is a constant in every job, every relationship, everything you do. THPL means never having to say three of the potentially most dangerous words in the English language:

"*I know that.*"

I have made a career of saying "I *don't* know that," followed quickly by, "How can I find out?" Through continuous learning, you will arrive at a state of "readiness" that enables you to respond fluidly, competently, and gracefully to almost any situation in which you might find yourself.

As my life stories illustrate, I have the firm belief that Fitness is the core of our physical and spiritual being.

We homo sapiens were originally designed to live on twigs, berries, nuts, and run 15-20 miles per day in search of meat. In today's "point-and-click" world, we are now capable of managing our entire existence from an armchair. Note I said "existence," which is not the same thing as *life*. Today, more than ever, we need to vigorously exercise our bodies to keep them in a state of wellness, strength, and flexibility. Bravo to everyone out there who has an exercise routine! Now how can you step it up? And if you're reading this without an exercise plan, don't you think you need one? Start small and work up. Your body will thank you.

A healthy heart is more than just cardiovascular efficiency. It's also a heart that both feels and feeds the world with compassion, connecting to the whole of our existence.

When you're living your version of The High Performance Life, your heart will open up your eyes, enabling you to see and do things differently. And The High Performance Life version of you will always be poised to take on new challenges and find untold levels of personal fulfillment.

By pure habit, we humans do everything that's required of our organism: we eat, we sleep, and we take care of our personal hygiene. People everywhere do these three things for obvious reasons. What differentiates the High Performance individual is these organic behaviors are now fully integrated with an elevated understanding of Life, Learning and Fitness…in a way that opens up a space for a truly fulfilling life, beyond what you could have ever imagined.

Here it is in summary:

THPL JOURNEY

LIFE (SOUL)	LEARNING (MIND)	FITNESS (BODY)
With positive emotions and a no-constraint mindset, we make well-balanced choices, and take well-guided actions, surrounded by a loving and supportive community.	Seeking information and knowledge that enables us to improve our behaviors, increase competencies, and achieve a maximum state of readiness.	Integrating physical and spiritual activity, combined with nutrition, into our daily lives, to create a mind/body/soul connection that is both healthy and powerful.

A Healthy, Capable, Present and Powerful Mind, Body & Soul

I'll say it once more. If you can…

Live in the Mystery…

Show up,

Believe in the Process,

And let go of your Expectations…

…Magic becomes real,

And Dreams come true,

As Power, Passion and Possibility conspire to unleash your version of

The High Performance Life.

It begins now.

Joe Gagnon 69

CHAPTER 6 –

Here's "How it Works"

(Thank you Bill W. and Dr. Bob)

To borrow a phrase from 12 Step Programs, *"It works if you work it."* This simple directive tells us that if we want to *be* better, we have to *do* better.

Your very ability to transform these letters into words, which then become thoughts and images, is due to the fact that you began training your brain to read before you ever entered school, and now you're an expert in it. But you had to work at it to get there.

Here's the point: If you want to change yourself, you must be willing to invest yourself in the effort. It makes no difference whether the transformation is physical, mental or spiritual. There is no "shining light" moment. Change will only happen if you expend the energy. Why wait? You can do this.

And the good news is that we humans are programmed to do this. We are literally learning machines, and you only have to look at an infant to see it in action. Just as babies go from large to small muscle movement, we learn best when we go from simple to complex. So, that is how this book is designed.

In the following pages, you will have the opportunity to begin the first of several exercises, each relating to a specific component of The High Performance Life. Just as THPL is "accumulative" by its nature, these activities build, one upon the previous. To get the fullest benefit, each of these exercises should be *fully undertaken* and *understood* before moving on to the next.

Important Note: If you hold yourself at arm's length from these challenges, though you may get temporarily inspired, you will not likely see lasting results in your life. However, if you *apply yourself*, and take on these challenges as if your life were at stake (because, let's face it, it is), you will find yourself living your own unique version of The High Performance Life! If you feel you are having trouble understanding or practicing an exercise, please contact us at *Joe@TheHighPerformanceLife.net*, and we will be happy to assist you, and invite you into our THPL Community.

Exercise – Who, What & Why?

There are two basic components of any journey: "WHERE?" (The destination) and "WHY?" (The reason).

Your "where" is completely personal to you, so I will not try and define it for you. In fact, you will be doing that for yourself shortly.

However, in order to answer "WHY?" you must first answer the question of "WHO" you are capable of being and "WHAT" you are willing to do about it.

For example, as you partake in this exercise you might discover WHO you are is a mystery not yet defined. For all we know, you could be a "rainmaker" here to break with convention, raise the bar, discover a higher possibility for humanity; be an inspiration to your family and friends; or be the best dad, mom, homemaker, marathoner, creator, contributor to society you can possibly be, etc.

NOTE: This and all exercises in this book should be done in *pencil*, or online at our website. Space is provided within the book for journaling, however if you have more to say than will fit in the allotted areas (*Bravo!*), please feel free to dedicate a separate journal to your THPL journey.

Exercise – Who Are You?

Write a list of ten brief present tense sentences (or adjectives) that define your best self. The worksheet below gives you a perfect start, for example: "I am grateful to be an inspiration to everyone I meet!"

I am _____

I am _____

I am _____

I am _____

I am _____

I am _____

I am _____

I am _____

I am _____

I am _____

Exercise – What Do You Want (And What Are You Willing to Do About It)?

1. Describe what your life would look like, sound like, and feel like if you were living your version of THPL?

   _____

   _____

2. What kind of results and outcomes would you like to achieve in your THPL?

   _____

   _____

3. What actions are you taking, or envision taking toward living THPL?

   _____

   _____

4. If you imagine creating the outcomes you desire, what would this do for your life?

   _____

   _____

Exercise – Why?

When you contemplate your "WHY", you activate your awareness of your purpose for being alive. In the spaces provided or in your journal, answer the following questions:

1. What is my higher life purpose?

   _____

   _____

2. When the going gets tough (which it absolutely will) why should I persist in sticking with my purpose?

   _____

   _____

3. How does my version of THPL impact the world around me?

   _____

   _____

4. Long after I'm gone, what will the ripple effect of my version of THPL journey be on future generations?

_____

_____

5. Who do I have to be in order to fulfill my version of THPL?

_____

_____

6. What habits do I need to change (or what do I need to let go of) in order to thrive in my version of THPL?

_____

_____

PART I I– LIFE

With positive emotions and a no-constraint mindset,

we make well-balanced choices

and take well-guided actions,

surrounded by a loving and supportive community.

Who wouldn't want this to be their life? And how many of us can truly claim that it is?

In this section we will explore the following topics:

Dream It, Plan It, Practice It, Do It

Becoming Ready

THPL Community

The Best Possible You

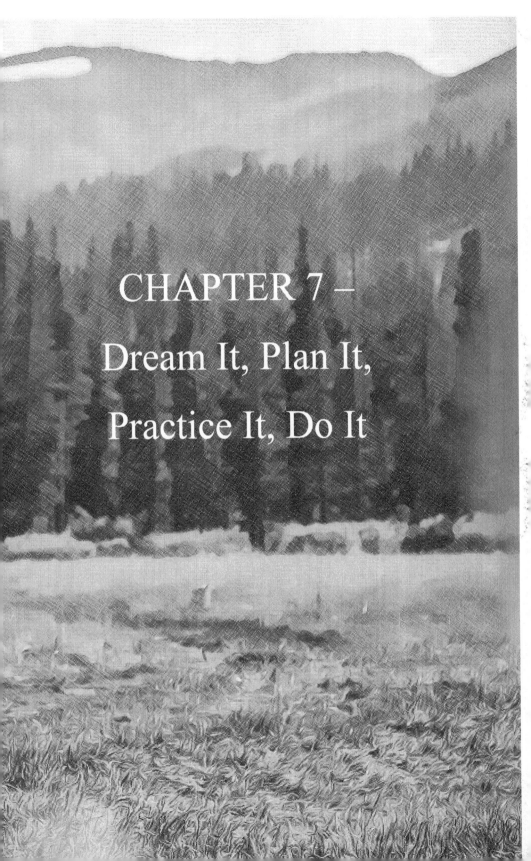

CHAPTER 7 –
Dream It, Plan It,
Practice It, Do It

There are four elements to accomplish anything. These are:

Dream It,

Plan It,

Practice It, and

Do It.

If you can succeed at all four, my experience has shown me that you can do things that will positively amaze you.

Dream It

Everyone dreams, but are we all using our dreams to their fullest potential? I'll bet not.

Our dreams are the catalysts for action. They are the wellspring of new realities for ourselves, with those we love and for everyone else around us. Our dreams become the foundation of our actions, precipitating the next step: *planning*.

In the dreaming stage you are given permission to access the "childlike" part of your mind, the part of you that thinks waaaaaaay outside the box and does not segregate the impossible from the possible. You don't need anyone's permission to dream. Give yourself the gift of thinking, imagining and dreaming of what might be your next challenge, or adventure. We all have this innate ability, but so few of us use it to its fullest potential. So, if you're going to dream, don't go halfway. Go all out!

Think about it this way: If anything was possible, if you had no limits, if you had nothing to fear, if money wasn't an issue, what would thrill you?

How might you challenge yourself?

What would you dare to dream for yourself?

Maybe you've read a story about someone who greatly inspired you and you thought,

"I bet I could do that!"

~ OR ~

"I wish I could do that."

~ OR ~

"How did he or she do that?"

Making your dreams a reality starts with how you dream, and there are ways to improve your dreaming effectiveness.

Exercise – Dream It

Take a few moments to write down all the
activities/challenges/aspirations you can dream for yourself
(aka your "bucket list"); those things you've always
dreamed you could, or should, do:

_____

_____

_____

_____

_____

_____

Now, choose one that truly lights you up, and makes you
feel like if you did it you'd be in the bull's eye of your
version of The High Performance Life. Write it down here:

_____

Now take it to the next level and, with your childlike
imagination running the show, envision yourself in your

dream as vividly as possible. In fact, envision the entire process.

Take a snapshot in your mind of the best moment in your dream. Bring in all your senses into this moment by asking yourself:

What do you see?

Where are you?
What colors or people are there?
What time of day is it?

_____

_____

How do you feel?

What emotional sensation are you feeling?
How does the wind/sun/water feel on your body?

_____

_____

What do you hear?

The sounds of nature? A crowd cheering? A song? Your

heart beating?

_____

_____

What do you smell?

Are there any particular fragrances that you notice?

What do you taste?

_____

_____

Go ahead and exaggerate this dream, make it larger than life, especially the "feeling tone," the emotional energy it creates. Emblazon that in your heart and your mind.

_____

_____

Now that your dream is alive within you, you are ready for the next step to help you make this a reality: *planning.*

Plan It

Planning is where dreams become reality. Having a dream without a plan is just that: a nice thought that vanishes on waking. It's fine to say, "I want to get my degree" or "I want to run a marathon."

Whatever your dream is, I wish you good luck with it, but it's not a *plan*. It's also a fine thing to have hope: for a better world, or for a friend in need. I can "hope" you're going to read the next sentence, but that won't guarantee it will happen. It is famously said that hope is not a strategy. And when it comes to actually getting things done, it's a non-starter.

The Chinese have another way of viewing it, in their proverb that says,

"You do or you don't do. There is no such thing as 'try."

In my personal story, my "plan" began forming in my Minnie Mouse years, and took fuller shape after "the Gary

Arm Wrestling Incident." As you've seen already, the very next day I began charting every one of my physical activities, a habit I still pursue to this day. And just like dreaming, one of the most persistent misconceptions we have about planning is that we somehow need *permission* to do it.

Question: Who's in charge of that for you?

Answer: you are.

You'll probably need to include others in your plan, but you have permission on behalf of me and the Universe to go ahead.

In 1985 I was working at Mercantile Stores, my second job. I was very excited because we were going to a "technology vendor presentation." I hadn't the vaguest notion of what this was, but it sounded important. In the presentation, there were at least 50 other people in the audience. Everyone in attendance seemed twice my age and way more experienced than me.

When they got to the Q&A, both the questions that were asked and the conversation that ensued seemed totally sophomoric to me. This caused me to wonder if it was possible that I actually knew more than these "experienced" employees.

I had only been on the job for a few months, but mainly because I didn't know any better, I had relentlessly applied myself to studying PC software. I didn't ask anyone if it was okay. I just did it in the belief that it would help me get ahead. The "other guys," relying on their years of experience, didn't put in anywhere near the same effort.

I began to realize that this disciplined effort and focus[7] gave me the ability to master a given topic and this would be to my advantage.

Throughout my career, I have made the realization that a great majority of the people in the world are content to be

---

[7] "Human potential experts think of the concept of cultivating extraordinary potential that its advocates believe to lie largely untapped in all people. The movement took as its premise the belief that through the development of "human potential", humans can experience an exceptional quality of life filled with happiness, creativity, and fulfillment. As a corollary, those who begin to unleash this assumed potential often find themselves directing their actions within society towards assisting others to release their potential. Adherents believe that the net effect of individuals cultivating their potential will bring about positive social change at large" – Wikipedia

like those "other guys." They're content to plod through life by being utterly average. That deadly sentiment "everything in moderation" drives them. They play to the middle, seeking to cause as little strain in their lives as possible. For them life is all about contentment.

I chose another path. And as I have traveled throughout my High Performance Life journey, I have found myself being almost always happy, but very seldom content, which gave rise to another one of my personal mottos:

Always happy, never satisfied.

Thinking about things in new ways springs from the realization that how I speak about my life changes the way I think about it.

Think about it. How you think can change how you feel. How you feel can change who you are. As you move along on your THPL path, it's a good idea to remind yourself that the only way to get to "there" is to go through the process that will take you from "here" to wherever else you'd rather be.

To help you get started, here are some words you can easily replace in your vernacular (feel free to add to this list from your own experience):

"Here"	**"There"**
I can't/won't	I can/will
There isn't	There is
They wouldn't	They could
Impossible	Possible
Why?	Why not?

Another enemy of planning is a failure to set milestones and deadlines. If your plan doesn't include definite and predictable outcomes with graduated steps along the way it becomes a huge and insurmountable obstacle. Far too many people don't climb to the top of mountains because they're intimidated by the hugeness and distance of the peak, instead of just taking the next step that's in front of them that will get them there.

Could you run a marathon tomorrow? Maybe not. Could you begin a process of exercise and diet that will bring you to that ability? Most definitely.

That fateful night when Gary pinned me I could not have envisioned the transformed life I live today. I just knew I wanted to get healthier and more physically ft. So, I set out a plan to get there.

I set out to run three miles and do a total of 100 pushups. I took it in bite sized pieces with lots milestones along the way, so I could see, feel, and celebrate my progress. And as for deadlines, I made them reasonable, but always slightly outside of my comfort level.

I employed techniques such as "just do one more." One more pushup, one more mile, one more minute, ten seconds quicker. You can say, "I want to do a mile in 10 minutes." Right now I'm at 15. Whatever the activity, just add a little bit more before you are done and steady progress will happen. You can count on it.

And for those big goals, such as running a marathon some might be inclined to say, "I'll never be able to do that." Of course you can't, *today*, especially if you've never done it before. But you can start running, training, practicing. It can be as simple as taking a walk and then a jog and then a run – it moves us in the right direction.

Organized runners know this. That's why there are many 5K and 10K events that allow participants to step up to longer distances and higher goals. And in this digital age, it's never been easier to set up a performance plan to help us track our progress.

There are dozens of wearable technology solutions[8] that come with their own software apps. You can become as involved in their "programs" as you like, but there are literally

---

[8] These include (but are not limited to) Fitbit, Garmin, Samsung Gear Fit, Apple Watch, and many others

dozens of ways to accurately track your progress digitally, which may well be vastly superior to the "analog" notebook I began in 1999. But that process worked because I *chose* to make it work. The real difference isn't the technology. It's you.

By setting milestones and deadlines, you now get to move onto the next phase, which is practicing: becoming more competent in the skills and more physically adept at using them.

Practice It

This is where we "pay our dues," and as such, it's another obstacle-rich environment. Let's be honest, there are a million ways to lose interest, ranging from it's too tough or painful, to it's too hard to fit into your schedule.

We cannot leave it there!

None of these so-called "reasons" are true excuses to not move forward. Fighting through the entropy that takes place when the body is at rest is possible as long as we focus on the goal (aka the WHY) and do the work that's necessary. Then, when we start to see progress, however hard that might feel to us at any one moment, we get a glimmer of inspiration.

By staying attuned to our vision for what is possible (our
dream),
We remain connected to inspiration we need to keep us
moving forward.

As you pursue The High Performance Life, I can promise this discovery:

You are capable of doing much more than you think you can.

Discomfort is another of the major obstacles we face. Starting out as crying babies in wet diapers, we've all known a million forms of discomfort. A runner in the final miles of a marathon experiences a level of discomfort that's nearly transcendental. We also have uncomfortable, even painful memories that can haunt us.

Let's be honest, many pain signals are there for good reason. They're our body's way of telling us we're hurt. But how many of us misinterpret mere signs of *discomfort* as pain, when they're really there to tell us we're taxing our bodies in a *good* way.

We also experience *external* discomfort in the form of people and surroundings. An irritating co-worker. A hot humid day. A snarky salesperson. Someone you're trying to avoid. Stuck in traffic. And that's all it is: pain or irritation, or fear, or regret.

Here's a thought:

What if we choose to <u>experience</u> discomfort rather than just enduring it?

What if we decide to accept it as a temporary condition with dimensions and capacities that provokes emotions both negative and positive?

I'll throw out the most extreme example I can think of: Navy Seals. They go to the most uncomfortable places and do impossible things at unimaginable times. Their whole training is built around exposing themselves to maximum levels of discomfort, so they can learn how to use their own abilities to *normalize it*. That's why they can still perform at the top level under any circumstance.

Experiencing discomfort as just another aspect of a given activity is what enables us to normalize it, just like those high-performing Navy Seals, but on our own terms. We expect it. It's no big surprise. It's just there.

It's important to normalize discomfort, because it is one of the major obstacles most people face in fitness. You *do* breathe harder. Your pulse raises. Your arms and legs *will* get tired and sore. And if you have any thought of improving your physical condition, you know that's a good thing! You also know that you will probably be even more sore the next day, but you stretch and you prepare, and you go on. And as hard as this may seem to believe, we can actually benefit from experiencing our discomfort!

If you're running on a cold rainy day, your hands and feet might get cold, your body may start to shiver. In that moment, you have two choices: you can either hate the discomfort, or you can *experience* it. Like any kind of work you do, you can transform it into a game. You can make room for it, accept it for what it is, and thus overcome it.

Let's be real clear: this is not about being a "tough guy (or girl)."
It is only about being able to rely on yourself to perform at a higher level
even when circumstances aren't perfect.

We're all used to lives that hopefully don't present us with routine challenges. But every so often life throws us a curve ball. Sadly, this seems to affect some people more than others, but none of us are immune. It could be a work or family challenge, even the death of someone close to you.

Whatever it is, it's the Universe telling us we need to level up. Accept life for all that it is, stand up to it, appreciate and embrace it, *don't run* from it. What's more, I maintain that any man or woman, *can* become tougher, without having to grow a thicker hide or losing one ounce of sensitivity. In fact, my experience has shown me that the truth is the exact opposite. Pain doesn't have to be traumatic or catastrophic. Plain old discomfort is also something we face in life. Uncomfortable situations are everywhere if we let them be.

My personal adventures have propelled me through too many of them to count.

What do I do when faced with discomfort?

First, I don't walk away (as my "Got the Tee-Shirt" story would indicate). But on that insane bike ride, the notion that *pain is temporary* and *quitting is forever* was etched in my brain. And it applies to much more than just quitting a race. When we quit in life we close a door.

> *There are always a million reasons to quit,*
> *and nearly 100% of them are invented by us.*

How about this? Instead of saying "I can't do that," say, "I can, and I will." Instead of saying "They won't let me," why not say "I'm not going to wait for permission." Being successful is almost always entirely within our control, so let's drop a weak defense and give a strong offense a try.

You've now explored: Dream It, Plan It and Practice It. What's left?

To quote Nike, "just do it." Don't try. Don't talk about it.

Do It.

168 Hours

If you multiply 24 hours x 7 days, you arrive at the mathematical result that is a total of 168 hours in every week. But how many of us look at that whole number?

Our typical focus is usually something like 40 hours of work, the 40 hours we have to ourselves and our families, and the 8 hours we ought to sleep (and often don't), which adds up to another 56 hours.

The first observation is those numbers only add up to 136! That means there are 32 remaining hours each week that we didn't account for! You can think of it as more than an extra day that you didn't even know you had!

What if we take a *full accounting* of how we're using every one of those 168 hours? Taking it a step even further,

168 hours = 10,080 minutes. Going any more granular than that might be a bit over the top. But what are you doing with those minutes? How many of them are idle or just plain wasted?

And isn't it possible that, even during periods of rest, we can be actively planning and preparing for future actions?

I believe that it is.

Exercise – My 168 Hour Life

In the space below, or on a sheet of paper, identify how you spend your 168 hours. Notice where you may be wasting time or where you have more time than you realized.

	Sunday	Monday	Tuesday	Wednesday	Thursday	Friday	Saturday
12:00 AM							
1:00							
2:00							
3:00							
4:00							
5:00							
6:00							
7:00							
8:00							
9:00							
10:00							
11:00							
12:00 PM							
1:00							
2:00							
3:00							
4:00							
5:00							
6:00							
7:00							
8:00							
9:00							
10:00							
11:00							

Exercise – Dream It, Plan It, Practice It, Do It!

Write down five THPL Dreams

1._____

2._____

3._____

4._____

5._____

Select one dream that feels the most important to you at this time (this will be, from this point forward, referred to as your THPL Breakthrough Goal):

1._____

Exercise – Dream It, Plan It, Practice It, Do It! (Part 2):

Create a step-by-step PLAN to accomplish it

1._____

2. _____

3. _____

What you will need to practice in order to realize this goal?

1._____

2. _____

3. _____

NOW – look back at your **168 Hour Life** Grid. What will need to change in order to make room for your THPL Breakthrough Goal?

CHAPTER 8 –
Becoming Ready

The real outcome of all your planning and preparation is that it enables you to live in the *ready state*. That means at any moment a challenge is handed to you, you are ready to take it on, because you've already prepared and practiced. No additional thought required.

Being in the ready state means that you are adaptable, flexible, able to take on whatever comes next. As much as we try to shape lives that are sensible, predictable and safe, life can be an adventure sport sometimes, and we have absolutely no control about what comes our way. The only thing we can control is how we react. And being ready means our reaction is of *our* choosing, not based on mere impulse.

Neurobiology is making huge inroads in our understanding of the brain's function. There is clear proof that the limbic brain (the same one we share with 99% of the rest of the creatures on this planet) is an essential "valve." Every input we receive or impulse we transmit must first pass through this single corridor, and the first and only question it asks is, "Will it kill me?" If the answer is "no," the rest of the brain is open for business as usual. If the answer is "Yes," a completely different set of biochemical responses is triggered, and for good reason. This "fight or flight" mechanism takes over your entire adrenal system giving you vast stores of new energy to tap, rerouting blood away from the surface so you'll bleed less if attacked, quickening your pulse and breathing so you'll be ready for action[9].

Our instinctive readiness traits helped us greatly tens of thousands of years ago when we faced existential threats on a daily basis, and they have been hardwired in us ever since. The plain fact is that most of us aren't being attacked by vicious beasts on a daily basis anymore, so we substitute being in traffic, or being approached by a stranger on the street for this same level of threat. And instead of becoming more able to respond we seem to go the other way: paralyzed by reactive fear.

---

[9] If you want to see the state of readiness on perfect display look at almost any dog. Those of you who own dogs, know exactly what I mean. Say the word "walk" and almost any canine of any age will spring immediately into action. And within just a few moments your dog will be confused as to why you aren't ready to go now, too, so you'd better be ready when you say the word.

Underpinning much of our fear is self-doubt: that "committee inside our head" that criticizes and limits us.

News break: Those voices are us!
They are entirely of our invention.
And the criticism?
You guessed it. We made almost all of that up, too!

Now what about doubt cast upon us by others? Being the highly imperfect creatures we are, there are times when we honestly need to hear the voices of constructive critics, especially if they're speaking from love and/or expertise in the matter. In these circumstances, we are well-served to listen to what they have to say and heed their advice where warranted.

But here's what I also know. Opinions can be greatly overrated because they can often be formed on such scant input. Your opinion of me isn't me. Similarly, my opinion of you isn't you. So, instead of disregarding the opinions of others, let's take them in dispassionately, examine them, and through practice, become more adept at distilling the useful from that which is better being tossed off. Then there are those moments when you can look at a person just once, and have an immediate knowledge that soars so far past "opinion" as to render the word meaningless.

This is the intuitive heart. Listen to it.
This is being in the ready state.

Being in a ready state, enables us to reprogram our thought processes to be much more flexible to a wider range of possibilities and available to a wider range of responses. I've already admitted to some of my eccentricities, especially when it comes to physical training. I run an average of 70 miles per week. I spend no less than 90 minutes every day exercising. Big deal. That's just what I feel works for me. The fact is that I could also give a presentation to a group of a thousand people at any given moment, because I've studied my content and I'm not just 100% familiar with it, I'm an expert, because I've done it dozens of times before. I've created that reality because I have practiced and prepared.

What's stopping you from living in a ready state?

NOTE: It's very important to not equate readiness with wariness. Many people feel that worrying about everything all the time means they're ready for it, when in reality, all they're ready for is for something bad or uncontrollable to happen. The ready state takes you out of fear.Being ready also means being rested. There are many advocates who admonish us for not getting enough sleep. Here's another area where I'll have to admit guilt. I sleep an average of five hours a night, but one self-imposed sleep barrier is my insistence on publishing my daily blog at exactly 3:00 AM Eastern Time US, regardless of where in the world I happen to be. I made that commitment in 2013 and I have not failed to execute it ever since. That's just how I'm wired and once again, I'll admit to being skewed from the norm.

There is also a big difference between sleep and rest. Because of my obsession with physical training, my body does require significant rest every day. But I think of rest periods as "active recovery." What if, even while resting, we can still remain mentally active? We never turn the machine completely off. We just let it cool down a little. That is a way to stay in a "ready state," even while recovering.

Exercise – What's Your Minnie Mouse?

In order to truly live in a ready state, we need to have "all systems go" within us. One of the biggest reasons people set goals that they don't fulfill is because of deep-seated fears and erroneous beliefs about themselves. We all have a potential "Minnie Mouse" in our closet, and if it hasn't been faced and embraced in the light of day the effect is equivalent to having one foot on the gas and one foot on the break.

What most people don't realize is that once our own personal "Minnie Mouse" has been embraced, or at least given room to roam outside the closet, great gifts are in store for us. The first is humility: the recognition that we're no better, or worse, than any other living soul on this planet. The next is compassion for the struggles of others. And the third is that we no longer subconsciously feel the need to sabotage ourselves.

Our ego's biggest terror is that we expose our vulnerabilities. If you want to live an ordinary life then play it safe. If, however, you want to live The High Performance Life, neutralizing your "kryptonite" is key.

So…what's the Minnie Mouse (the thing you are ashamed of, don't want people to know about you, or your biggest challenge) in your closet?

Describe it here:

_____

_____

What happened?

_____

_____

How much did it hurt? Why?

_____

_____

What did it teach you? How?

_____

_____

Is it still running your life? Why?

_____

_____

How can you turn your Minnie Mouse into your *Mighty Mouse*?

_____

_____

CHAPTER 9 –
THPL Community – The
Essential Connection to
Our Humanity

The High Performance Life is nonexistent without a loving and supportive community around us. At the purest levels of sociobiology, our family is our core community, extending outward to our friends, co-workers, acquaintances and ultimately everyone else in the world.

The family that we were born into is first, and then many of us go on to create families of our own. I cherish my family, but I will also be honest and admit that I was a "virtual parent" much of my life. The demands of my career meant that my supportive wife Anthea, despite her career aspirations, had to be willing to be the "at-home" parent to our two daughters, Kimberly and Julianne.

I will readily admit that it was tough to be away from them. In spite of the fact that I would swoop in as often as I could, I certainly missed enough important milestones to be sure, and the little everyday things too. A favorite story at bedtime followed by a goodnight kiss, bandaging a skinned knee, wiping away a tear. These are things you just can't replace. For these reasons, I reached out to them continually, calling every day, then texting when that became available.

And I didn't call just to chat. I called to *connect*, to find out what was important to them that day, and to let them know that they were deeply loved. We talked about missing each other, and ways that we could "normalize" our circumstance and come to greater peace with it.

We dreamed, made plans, and practiced, so that we could make the most of our upcoming times together. And traveling as much as I did made those moments that much more precious, so I learned early on not to waste one second of our togetherness.

And my wife? She loves tennis, but every time I was home she would ask, "Do you mind if I go play?" 10,000 times she asked me that, and I'm hard pressed to think of a single occasion when I said "no." It's not about getting permission. Rather, it is a way of showing respect. That's just one way we take care of our most essential THPL community.

Even when I was only commuting to New York City from my suburban home, I tried to make use of the two hours I spent in traffic every day. I would listen to books on tape in the car. I would try my best to use that time to defuse emotions that may have built up during the day, and strategize about how to best approach the day(s) ahead.

And if I was still out of sorts when I got home, I would try my best to quietly announce that fact and beg everyone's permission to be by myself for a little while and decompress. If I was met with a sink full of dirty dishes, instead of grumbling about "Why are these here?" I learned to just clean them, quietly and pleasantly. I learned to make that a gift to my overworked spouse. I used the time to talk to the girls and make plans for activities.

Exercise – Two Words That Can Be Never Be Overused

My anniversary cards to my wife are always "thank you" cards. And I try to say thank you at least ten times a day to those who cross my path. Who needs to hear a "thank you" from you?

Saying thank you is a way of expressing gratitude and humbling yourself to the knowledge that as cool as you might think you are, you can't do life alone. Why would you even want to try? The only thing you can do is to bring your best self to the game. And that's because we can't do life, much less *The High Performance Life*, by ourselves.

So now you can list *at least 10 people* who deserve to get a "thank you" from you. What will you thank them for?

1. _____
2. _____
3. _____

4. _____

5. _____

6. _____

7. _____

8. _____

9. _____

10. _____

11. _____

Accountability Partner(s)

As we proceed along our THPL pathway, it never hurts to have someone who shares your dreams, understands your plans, and is willing to get in there and practice with you. I call this an "Accountability Partner," but you can call him or her anything you like.

And of course, you fulfill a symbiotic role for your accountability partner, too. You may already know this person, and if you're not sure where to look, they're probably hiding in plain sight among your family, friends and co-workers.

As you follow on your THPL path, that community will grow. Similarly, we need to be aware of "failure friends," those people who are in our lives and for whatever reason, cannot or will not go along with you toward positive goals. These are the folks who tell you, "You can't..." or "You shouldn't..." or "You won't..."

First: they aren't your friends.

Second, they don't know squat.

And third, you get to choose whether you allow them in your life or not.

Many people encounter "failure friends" inside of working environments or their own dysfunctional families where it is much harder to escape, and still we must find a way to disallow their unqualified, ignorant, self-serving behavior, all without making them feel even worse about themselves. Sadly, that could take up another book entirely.

Exercise – The Best Possible You

You will probably end up being an amalgam of the five best people you've ever known, at any point in your life. These are the people who matter, who personify the behaviors and attitudes you choose to emulate. They are in the dead center of your High Performance Life community.

Who are the *five best people* you've ever known? List them here:

Next to each person's name, write one word that describes what you most admire about them (i.e. confident, empowering, uplifting, adventurous, successful, spiritual, reassuring, affirming, bold, innovative, eloquent, nurturing, trailblazing, generous, change-maker, exciting, eloquent, reliable, etc.)

1. _____

2. _____

3. _____

4. _____

5. _____

Now put your left hand over the left side of the page (covering the names) and see the 5 qualities that describe the best possible version of *you*!

Transforming Community

Accountability can be both personal and professional. One of my recent jobs was as President of Penn Foster, a 125-year-old institution that has transformed over the years from a traditional "correspondence school" to being completely online. My first week on the job, I took it upon myself to get out onto the "shop floor," as it were.

Our contact center was staffed by hundreds of "enrollment advisors" whose job was to explain the courseware to potential students and help them register. They followed very rigid scripts which gave them very little "conversational leeway" with the prospect. And their results, while good, were far from great. They were meeting established business targets, but it always seemed like a stretch to get there. What hit me even more was their morale. Again, not as bad as a galley ship, but not a place of glowing enthusiasm either (and they knew they were performing for the boss!) It struck me that for these folks, this was just a "job," not a career, and certainly not a calling. And I could only imagine how it struck potential students on the other end of the line.

This experience prompted me to rethink the whole process. What if we gave our people more of a career focus? What if we helped them to realize that their "job" enabled them to change peoples' lives, and realize their career goals?

That's exactly what we did: we handed out shirts that said, "I'm a dream maker," and "I'm a life changer." Supervisors were now coaches. Isolated cubicles morphed into team neighborhoods. We threw out the scripts and sought instead a real conversation with real people about their dreams and goals and then worked backwards toward which program would be their best fit. Almost the next day, enrollments increased about 20%, and that success was not short-lived.

What had we done? We changed their accountability, from "sell" to "advise." We helped them to think of themselves differently, and we encouraged them in every way we could to help one another do the same. The Penn Foster community was able to achieve tremendous bottom line *business* results, because we focused on *human* results.

We also strengthened the Penn Foster community in other ways. Being that our classes were 100% "virtual," we would not ordinarily get to meet the students. I love students, and some of my happiest times have been spent in schools at every level. But because of our business model, we did not get to spend any real face to face time with them.

We operated out of a location in Pennsylvania, and I got it into my head that we should invite our students to come to the facilities for a meet and greet with the staff. Then I really got on a roll and decided to expand on this idea, by leading a bike ride to go out and meet students.

That was the birth of the "Choose to be more" tour. Just three of us at first, in matching bike kits, pedaling from Scranton, to Allentown, Philadelphia, Trenton, Newark and finally, right across the heart of Manhattan to Brooklyn. Our intent was to bring life and vitality back into the school, and improve our connection with our students by meeting them where they lived, in their communities, with their families.

Before taking off on the first leg, I told my fellow riders, "I don't know what we're about to find, but I'm sure it will be magical." And boy was it! As we went along, the word spread to other locations we hadn't visited yet and by the final stop in Brooklyn, we had almost 70 students show up on a Saturday to sit down and talk with us about their life dreams.

Magical indeed.

For what are you willing to hold yourself accountable? And who do you know who is willing to become your partner in that effort?

Exercise – What's Your New Job Title?

Give yourself a new title and share it with your accountability partner. Address each other by your new title.

Some examples are:

Life Changer

Change Maker

Super Hero

Wonder Woman

Rainmaker

Trailblazer

Dream Maker

Magic Creator

Earth Shaker

What will your new title be?

_____

_____

_____

_____

Exercise – Accountability Partner (Part I)

Identify five people who are supportive of you:

1. _____

2. _____

3. _____

4. _____

5. _____

- Reach out to each of them – explain what you're up to and ask for their help – if they cannot enthusiastically agree, thank them and move on.
- If they do agree, first find out what you can do to help them in return.
- Develop a small but dependable group of people who will become your accountability partners.

Exercise – Accountability Partner (Part 2)

Identify what support you need from each of the people who support you:

_____

_____

_____

_____

_____

Keep in mind, if you only get one person to agree to be your accountability partner, you are well on your way to living your version of THPL.

CHAPTER 10 –

The Best Possible You

Everything in The High Performance Life is geared toward a singular goal:

To enable you to be the best possible you that you can be.

You are in competition with no one else, unless you choose to be. It isn't about being faster or smarter than anyone else. It's about being faster and smarter than you were yesterday, and to be better tomorrow. It's a journey that takes you from where you are right now to where you might only dream you can be some day.

When you take these simple skills, and apply them to your life, you will become a better version of yourself, day by day, until one day in the not-too-distant future you will be able to look yourself in the mirror and say, "I am doing my best."

People often use those words (*"I'm doing my best"*) as an excuse. What if it was a statement of *fact*? What if you could say it and truly mean it?

*Important **Note:*** *None of this will work if you are using it to improve your bragging rights or gain an edge over someone else. And none of it matters unless you are entirely willing to freely share it with others.*

Self-interest has never served me, not once, and it will not serve you either. Just look at any of the great leaders in both the public and private sectors. The best of them gave more than they got. This "servant to life" mindset is critical to achieving THPL.

One of the best ways I've found to become a "servant to life" is to be a "pacer" for someone else. I did this with Brian, a good friend of mine, during the Leadville 100-mile trail run in Colorado. This guy was no novice. He'd already run the Ironman eleven times, so his endurance and his athletic abilities were not in question. But he'd never run a 100-mile race on foot, which is a totally different beast both technically and physically.

Then there's the peculiarities of the Leadville course. It's beautiful, but being in the heart of the Rockies takes away a lot of its bucolic charm. To begin with, the race starts at an altitude of 10,000 feet, and it's on an uneven trail (as opposed to a smooth road), with vertical climbs to almost 13,000 feet, where getting enough oxygen can be a problem for anyone.

To say that one's body reacts in funny ways to a race of this type is a massive understatement. The grades, both up and down, also wreak havoc on quads and ankles. The altitude wreaks havoc with hydration, affecting the gastrointestinal system. I won't go into any further detail here and let your imagination fill in the possibilities, but it can be most unpleasant. It is a race of survival.

To put it into even more quantifiable terms, an average of 50% of starters never complete this race (compared to a "normal" marathon where 9 out of 10 usually finish). It's that hard.

As Brian's pacer my whole outlook shifted. Instead of thinking about my personal needs, I was taking responsibility for his success. I changed my accountability from *my* goals, to *his*. I was there to "pull," not "push," to encourage, to support, to enable, and help him finish. It was that simple.

Having already completed the race two years earlier, I was in a perfect position to pace for Brian, because I understood what it would feel like, and I could tell what was normal and what wasn't. So, I could say to him, it's okay how you feel now because you'll feel better in a little while. Of course, not all of my coaching was "good news."

At one point, he wanted to hear that we were closer to the next checkpoint. I said, "No, it's going to take us a while." He grunted back, "Why can't you say something positive?" "I am," I said, "I'm actually trying to make sure that you hang in there long enough because if you think it's going to happen sooner, you're going to actually be in a more miserable state."

It isn't always about just happy news, right? Sometimes realism is important, and I'm thankful that Brian also realized later on, after battling with a fair amount of wishful thinking that he would suddenly blink and the race would be over. You can dream all you want, but it's not over until you cross the finish line. There's no short cut.

Once again, I've plucked another "extreme example" out of my personal history but I use it only to illustrate a lesson that can apply to anything we do. How often do we reach that point of discomfort that we just think we can't endure any longer, and quit? And we quit, when if we just looked inside ourselves and said, "That's not all I've got," we could push through to the other side, where it will in fact get better.

Some people's tolerance for pain and discomfort might be higher, but we all experience turning points like this and the choices we make in these moments can be life-altering.

There is also a real difference between *discomfort* and true *pain*. If you are injured or in danger of being so, *please don't be like me and keep on going.* A constant or recurring pain could mean it's time to visit the doctor. Or it might just mean that you need to do an activity differently.

We're not just talking about physical pain here.
Emotional pain can be just as devastating.

Try this: If you're experiencing tough times, ask yourself, "How am I right now, this very moment?" In other words:

Is a bus about to hit you?
Are you actually dying?
Is a real Tyrannosaurus Rex chasing you?

If the answer is "no" congratulations! You're okay! But more often than not our state of being is controlled by our own minds.

Ask yourself:

Are you regretful?
That's past and you can't do anything about it.
Are you fearful?
That's the future and you can't do anything about it...
...Other than to be ready if and when it does.

Most of our fear is just concocted by us anyway. Let's stop that.

Finishing off the race with Brian, I had done about 40 miles, and he finished the full 100! We were both exhausted, but exhilarated at the fact that he had achieved this incredible personal milestone. And me? Funny. I got way more than I gave.

This "servant to life" mindset is responsible for some of my fondest memories. Looking back on my experiences with Penn Foster, I might have had the term "President" hanging on my office door, but when I experienced the magical shift in behavior and attitude in our workforce, I became the servant. And on that *Choose to Be More* bike ride, instead of the master, I became the student.

Don't you find that to be true as well when humbling yourself in a service experience? You experience transformative energy in its purest state.

What ends up happening in all of this is the creation of a strong connection to the community around us. Imagine yourself on a crowded subway car, stuffed with people you don't know. You can choose to feel hemmed in, claiming that your "personal space" is being trampled. Or you can choose to focus attention on each and every other living being in that space, with compassion and empathy, never judging them because of how they look; rather imagining them all to be the perfect beings we all are.

We as a society have somehow created these false barriers, and we as individuals are the only ones who can take them down.

The other thing that ends up happening is a transformation inside of us.

We start showing up.

We deliver on our promises and commitments.

We support others.

We give of ourselves.

If people validly question us, we hold ourselves answerable

to them.

And if they're simply detractors, we remember that we've turned our "Minnie Mouse" into "Mighty Mouse." We don't need their approval, and therefore they don't have any power over us.

As if watching a foreign film, we can also read the "subtitles" and interpret the underlying truth of what they're saying, which might be,

"I'm scared because I've never dared to have such a life.

Even though I've been cast in the role of a cynic, I'm hoping
you'll prove me wrong.
I'm secretly rooting for you."

More often than not, we move forward on the road of life in the company of those who love us, who encourage us and believe in us. And we believe in them too, because that's the magic of the human connection.

Together, we become the best possible us that we can be.

Now imagine spreading it out into the community around us. What if this was a global phenomenon? Our world, and we as a people, face unprecedented challenges right now, and it will take all of us, with a focused energy, to navigate the future.

What if, instead of decline and disintegration, the "new normal" became ascent and connection? The only person in the world who can do anything about any of this is you, and as we've established, you can't do this alone. But we've also established that you can do it.

Let's remember, natural disasters aside, almost every crisis in our world today is "man-made." I submit therefore, that we can *re-make* it in our own, better, way.

> **Important Note:** *This is not a quid pro quo. None of this will work if you are expecting something in return. No pat on the back. Not even a thank you. You must be willing and able to give selflessly and unconditionally to the act and the individual(s).*

When you master this you will be amazed at the results.

Exercise – Servant to Life

Revisit the first exercise at the bottom of chapter 1 (Who Are You?) and consider how being a servant to life fits in with your vision of who you are.

Write your insights about this in the spaces provided (or in your THPL journal):

_____

_____

_____

_____

_____

_____

_____

To Consider:

- Did you already include service in your description?

- If no, why not? If yes, how will you incorporate service to become your Best Possible You?

_____

_____

_____

_____

_____

_____

_____

_____

PART III –
LEARNING

PREFACE

Seeking information and knowledge that enables us to improve our behaviors, increase competencies, and achieve a maximum state of readiness.

In this section we will explore the following themes:

Curiosity

Believing In the Process

Work VS. Play

Ready State: Deployment

CHAPTER 11 –

Curious and Curiouser

(Thank you, Lewis Carroll)

One of the keys to the survival of the human race is our extreme adaptability to learning. And one of our most important learning behaviors is curiosity: that nagging desire to know more, to find out why things happen and what we can do to alter the outcomes.

I have had the opportunity to marvel at the human potential for curiosity through the lens of fatherhood, watching my two daughters grow from infancy into vibrant women. My wife and I shared responsibility for the early years, but as my career expanded, she became the more hands-on parent. As they grew, during those precious times together, I reveled in my fatherly duties to teach them to swim, skate, bike, and ski.

And I threw in one more activity just for good measure: *rock climbing*.

Now before you start wagging a finger of disapproval, this was always done in the utmost of safety with proper equipment and coaching, graduating slowly toward more "technical" climbing. And yes, they did fall and get banged up a bit but thankfully never seriously.

We climbed as often as we could, wherever we could, inside, outside. Eventually we climbed Devils Tower in Wyoming, Joshua Tree in California, and Rocky Mountain National Park in Colorado. As they grew, we graduated from the simpler to the more difficult climbs.

My basic reasoning for introducing my girls to rock climbing so early was because, as I've discovered, it's *much harder to learn* activities like this when you're older. Good and strong communication and support skills are also easier to develop at an early age. If you acquire all of these skills early, you become a much better, more intuitive climber, as I can also attest, just by watching my daughters grow up. Today, I'm proud to say they both climb better than I can.

But an even more fundamental reason was to teach them to overcome one of the biggest barriers to curiosity: taking risks. Climbing gave them the ability to see opportunities that might present themselves as obstacles at first, and through experimentation and skill development, to overcome them.

This ability to take calculated risks means that you can be the one who steps ahead, especially when others are standing back. My years at Ernst & Young were a tremendously exciting time for me and for the company. We were dramatically expanding our basic accounting and tax consulting business, using our empirical knowledge of our clients' business to become their strategic consultants, a real transformative exercise for all concerned.

In this kind of flux, a tremendous opportunity was always just a meeting away. In my second year, I was lucky enough to be in the room when one of the partners told a group of us about our first "reengineering" project that was about to kick off at tech giant Xerox in Rochester, New York. This was a massive opportunity: to help redesign a Fortune 100 company, but also a massive unknown.

Right after that meeting broke up, I went into the office of the partner in charge and told him I wanted the assignment. He asked me what experience I had. I told him I didn't have any, but no one else at the company did either. I said I would make it my passion to go there and learn and do the best I possibly could. And I would not let him down[10].

I spent nine months working at Xerox World Headquarters in Rochester NY. By the time I was done, I had helped transform core aspects of how they approached their business, and had earned the admiration of my company as well.

Another one of the biggest barriers to curiosity is our own stubborn unwillingness to admit we don't know something. The venerable Abraham Lincoln once said,

"It's better to remain silent and be thought a fool, than to speak out and remove all doubt."

---

[10] As it turns out, I was the only one who volunteered. Had I not, they would have picked someone from the staffing pool. But because I volunteered they put me on it.

With all due respect to our 16th President, what if we flip that on its head and say,

"It's better to open your mouth and risk being thought a fool,
than to remain silent, and ensure you will remain one?

Three of the most blessed and powerful words in the English language are

"I don't know."

Especially when followed by,

"But I'm going to find out."

Aside from letting some air out of your ego balloon, admitting you *don't* know gives you the freedom to seek counsel from those around you who *do*. It's not about being wrong. It's about "getting it right," whatever "right" is, rather than being right for the prideful sake of it. Right in the purest form. Right with your fellows. Right with the Universe and the world around you.

And once again, this is a team effort. If you don't know and someone else does, it's your duty to ask. Similarly, if you know and someone else doesn't, it's your duty to share. Sharing knowledge is fundamental to the human experience, so it doesn't just benefit you to ask; it benefits the person you're asking as well.

If you're uncomfortable, preface it by saying,

"This might sound silly, but..."

Then swallow your pride, dial back your ego and ASK.

If there is a downside to curiosity, it's that you do occasionally risk disappointment. Having finished undergraduate school at Fordham University in the Bronx NY, I decided that the way to get on the fast track was to earn an MBA. Of course, the cost of tuition was extreme, but I kept on researching (remember this was years before the founding of Google) and found a program at the Australian School of Management, in Sydney, that would school me tuition-free if I could qualify.

There were only six spots available and out of hundreds of applicants, I was one of those chosen! I was in heaven, until I started filling out the registration forms which clearly indicated that I had just one responsibility: to purchase a round-trip plane ticket to Australia, retail cost at the time approximately $6,000.

It might as well have been six million! Sheesh, the whole reason I applied to this program was because I didn't have any money! Discouraged, but not done, I asked my parents if they could help. Sadly, they told me the money just wasn't there.

I wore this failure around like a wet hoodie sweatshirt for quite a while, but when I was offered an opportunity to enroll in an advanced programming class at work, my shattered disappointment quickly transformed into focused excitement. The skills I gained proved every bit as valuable to my career as that MBA would have been. And the people I met through that one class have also been instrumental in my career achievements.

So even when you hear "no," that roadblock can turn into a new road all its own.

As I said, I was lucky to be at the real pioneering edge of the Information Age, a time when our curiosity has never been easier to indulge. I fondly remember when I was in high school how the 1959 World Book Encyclopedia was a permanent fixture in our living room, thirty or more separate volumes that contained the sum total of all human knowledge. I used to spend hours poring through the pages of World Book in an endless fascination with the sheer volume of information it held.

In the days when computers took up entire rooms, this was state of the art information technology. Today we can hold billions of times that amount in the palms of our hands.

They really are marvelous devices, these smartphones, and even as I write this, I know the term "smartphone" will itself probably be obsolete in a few years.

What is truly transformative about the age we live in is all of this "information" is now available to nearly anyone on earth, creating tremendous potential for good. The challenge to us is to sort out what's worth knowing from what isn't, to discipline yourself in how you pursue real knowledge versus trivial information, or worse, *mis*information that's either the cause of negligence or downright malevolence.

Look back at your 168 Hour Life chart one more time. Are you *really* accounting for all the unproductive time you spend in front of a screen? Do the words "cat videos" resonate?

That said, there's a tremendous Universe out there to know about. And your curiosity is the key to finding it.

Exercise – Curious and Curiouser

For most people on the planet, the default mode = "I know that."

- "I don't know" can make us phobic – or it can inspire us to action.
- Curiosity makes not knowing it all a pleasure

Identify 10 things about which you would be curious if there were no limits on time or money.

1. _____

2. _____

3. _____

4. _____

5. _____

6. _____

7. _____

8. _____

9. _____

10. _____

- Circle one thing upon which you will take action.
- Revisit your 168 Hour matrix and look for slots to plug in the time you will devote to indulging your curiosity.
- Share your curiosity with your accountability partners and seek to know theirs.

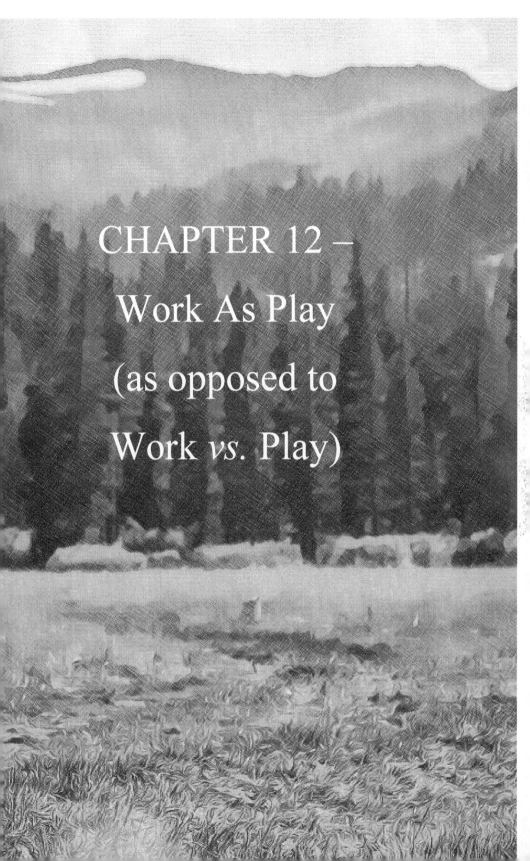

CHAPTER 12 –

Work As Play

(as opposed to

Work *vs*. Play)

I've held ten positions in all[11]. As you've already heard, some of them have been tremendous and some less so. Some, like McDonalds, were downright painful. But one fact unites them all.

Every single job I've had has been an <u>incredible</u> learning experience.

I mean why else would you show up? Of course, the obvious reason is they pay you. And it is entirely possible that we all have had a share of less than perfect jobs. But think back: did you not learn something from each and every one, even if it was the fact that you'd definitely never ever work there again?

Just a couple of centuries ago 99% of all work was purely physical. The Industrial Revolution took huge strides in having machines do the really backbreaking and dangerous jobs, but humans were still vital to the process. Today's

---

[11] For a complete curriculum vitae, please turn to Appendix A

technology is rapidly making physical labor obsolete, leaving us with a future that we could either view dimly or not.

The dim view is all that will be left are menial service jobs. The more optimistic view is the job market will morph into something we've never seen before, with more jobs requiring more creativity and inventiveness and an ability to rapidly transform ourselves.

There never was a better time to live The High Performance   Life.

Every job is a potential University: an opportunity to acquire new skills and abilities, and also to acquire greater knowledge of yourself. Admittedly some jobs may teach you more than others, but every time you face a new responsibility, learn a new skill, take on a new challenge, you are growing, learning, becoming a more competent version of you.

Every job is also an opportunity to not just do *well*, but also an opportunity to do *good*. My father's calling as a Social Worker enabled him to do a whole lot of "good" for those he served. And he did it at a wage that gave us a good, while never an affluent, life. *We lived well.*

Choosing to try for higher earnings, I took the corporate route. However I still view myself as a "social worker" in every setting. I try to make the surroundings the best they can be by being the best that I can be. And by doing that, I bring out the best in those who are around me.

That's one thing all my occupations have had in common: a close proximity to people and how they live. I've seen them in restaurants, retail, academic, and corporate settings. I've participated, practiced, touched and felt. And the closer I got, the better it worked.

In 2006, I was the CEO of Exit 41. The product we sold was online ordering software for fast casual and casual dining restaurants with a call center to process orders. One of our largest customers was La Madeleine, a French bakery café that began in Texas and is now nationwide.

When we first got the account, I took it upon myself to visit La Madeleine and sample their products to get a feel for what it was they were selling. While I enjoyed everything on the menu, nothing impressed me more than their tomato basil soup. It is amazing, velvety, rich tomato taste with a hint of cream and basil.

As the account was up and running, I periodically listened into the calls our people were answering. It became clear to me that instead of selling a premium culinary experience, they were just "processing orders." How could they know how good the food they were "processing" was unless they actually tasted it?

So, we ordered five cases of tomato basil soup and had them shipped into the call center – this way the agents could try it and experience it. We asked them how they would describe it now. Bottom line, sales of tomato basil soup doubled.

Important Note: None of these business results occurred because of any divine inspiration or business genius on my part.

They came about because I took it upon myself to learn what my clients were selling, what made people like it, and then make logical conclusions based on that knowledge. Just as I have done repeatedly throughout my life, I turned work into a learning experience, and I leveraged that learning to help me, and my co-workers, achieve better results.

Another Important Note: I did not always learn these lessons while I was actually on the job.

Some took me decades to realize, and only now do I feel confident enough in the truth of what I'm saying to lay it out in these black and white terms, while fully acknowledging every shade of gray in between.

I'm a work in progress, and as time goes on, less and less I'm able to say, "I could have, should have, would have, but didn't."

Engaging in life is about feeling it, living it, experiencing it. We cannot know unless we do, and on our THPL journey, that is exactly what we set out to do, again and again, every day!

Albert Einstein once said, "A person who has never made a mistake never tried anything new." I've been wrong many, many times, but every one of these potential "failings" has taught me something I could never have learned in any other way. Just as I have learned to experience discomfort, I have come to embrace the fact that, if I can learn from them, mistakes can be a *gift*.

Throughout my professional life, I've also indulged my curiosity by asking lots of crazy questions[12]. I've made it a habit to spot patterns and trends, so I could try to predict

---

[12] One summer I went to 85 different Walmart stores to understand what went on there.

how things might change over time. To do that I've had to come to a deep understanding what my customers and employees really need, and differentiating that from what they think they want. In the business setting, the dynamic between these "needs" versus "wants" dictates human behavior.

Now think about your own life: What do you want? How does that contrast with what you truly need? How does one support the other?

We can never overestimate the value of good fortune either. And in that regard, I know that not everyone has had it as good as I have.

I had a tremendous upbringing, with true role models as parents. I was a young white male in a culture dominated by white males, I got to attend college, and I was fortunate enough to be in the right place at the right time during some of the most exciting and dynamic periods in U.S. economic history. And just like almost everyone else, I had to endure tough times like 9/11 and the crash of 2008.

What's molded me throughout this process is this growing idea that I could make any job into something better than what it presented me. They say "do what you love." I'm enough of a realist to know that isn't always possible. So I say instead, "love what you do" even if I've occasionally had to force myself to do it at first.

If I was pushing a broom in the back rooms of McDonalds, I was determined to be the best darned broom pusher in the world. If I was the CEO I was going to find out what made my business tick, from the ground up.

Do you have "jobs" in your life that you just hate? This doesn't have to mean hourly or salaried work. It can be the jobs you routinely do around the house and in your community. Why don't you see if you can transform those activities into something new, something which adds meaning and value to an otherwise forgettable experience?

This desire to make every act that I can, the best I can make it, is key to living The High Performance Life.

What have you learned from the jobs in your past?
What can you be learning from your current job?

As I matured in my career, my "Dream It, Plan It, Practice It, Do It" methodology took shape and it brought me continuous success. So many of my peers were just as ambitious as I was, but many of them didn't have my same disciplined focus or appetite for risk. They knew (or thought they knew) they wanted the corner office, but were unwilling to sometimes just put in the legwork that it took to get there. The risks, as they turn out are mostly theoretical, not real. Many people tend to over-dramatize the downside, which keeps us from realizing that we can affect most of the upside. By being engaged in this way, we create the ability to change the outcome. I am sure that if you do a bit of soul searching you will find examples of this in your life. Now, how can you do it more often?

Here's an idea: let's say you want to open a bakery. Why not get a job as a baker's assistant, so you can really understand the business from the bottom up, inside and out? If you want to design roads and bridges, get a job on one of the crews that has to go out and maintain them year-round. It's about humbling yourself to the experience, so you can grasp its totality.

It's about learning the job from the inside out, the ground up. Then, maybe you're ready to try for the job that might eventually lead to the corner office. And once you get there, maybe, just maybe, the view from inside the corner office isn't as great as you thought. This happened to me at Ernst & Young, where I had already "made partner" along with a seven-figure salary, after only six years at the firm.

Heading into my seventh year with the firm, I was perceived as a rising star, and they sent me to Italy as a keynote speaker for a group of a thousand people. Now here I was, having achieved the success I was convinced I wanted: A terrific job with a limitless future. A great house, fancy car, a great family. What's not to like?

After I got checked into the hotel, I hired a local guide to take me out rock climbing. He spoke almost no English and my Italian is pretty awful too, so there wasn't a whole lot of conversation between us. That turned out to be an amazingly good thing, because I got a lot of time to think as we climbed.

And right there, on the side of this rock, about two hours before I'm supposed to give one of the most important talks in my career, the thought that hit me in the back of my head was,

"You know boy, you are in the greatest rut of your life.
A lot of people would kill to be where you are, but is this all
there is?
There has to be more life yet to live."

Within six months I took on a leadership role in a subsidiary we were launching building a startup called ConnectedHealth.net. With about $10 million in capital we set out into the "Wild West" days of the dot.com revolution, when the Internet seemed to make anything possible. The right idea could make you a billionaire[13].

And we thought we had a tremendous idea: a platform that would curate and track medical health data and make it available to healthcare providers via the Internet[14]. With a team of fifty developers working on the project full time, we were making real progress and doing real things. It was just about the most fun one could have. It was at this moment I realized that the other rewards you got when you took on something risky, different and unknown were much more rewarding than just a paycheck.

My goal wasn't to be "the boss." It was to be the servant of my employee's needs. We worked around the clock, so I was in charge of making sure we had enough food and drink on hand so we could keep working. Best of all, I wasn't just a functionary inside of a huge machine. I was

---

[13] Just look at Bill Gates, Mark Cuban, Elon Musk and many others who turned concepts into piles of cash.

[14] If any of that sounds familiar, it's because that's what WebMD was able to do successfully.

leading a team that was creating something unique, something that truly had our personal stamp on it.

It also brought me another realization, and it revolves around that word I dislike so much:
Quitting.

There are obvious times in our lives when we want, or need, to quit. A bad job. A wrong turn. A lost relationship. It happens. There are times when the only smart choice is to quit.

There's a huge difference between running <u>away</u> from something we fear,
and running <u>toward</u> something out there that's way better.

In the vast majority of cases, I choose the latter. What about you?

One of my mentors once told me, "You'd better celebrate on your way to success boy, because you're never going to really get there." While my first impulse might have been to say, "I'll show you," I have come to realize the truth of what he said.

Even today, I can wave a very thick resume in your face, but can I truly say that I've achieved "success" in its fullest? How would I even know what that looked like? I've come to realize that life is a marathon, not a sprint, and every mile I cross is another reason to feel good. I have enjoyed many successes, and celebrated each and every one in one form or another. I hope you will do the same. Set your milestones and pat yourself on the back for achieving them. Share your successes with your THPL community and celebrate their successes as well, compounding the energy.

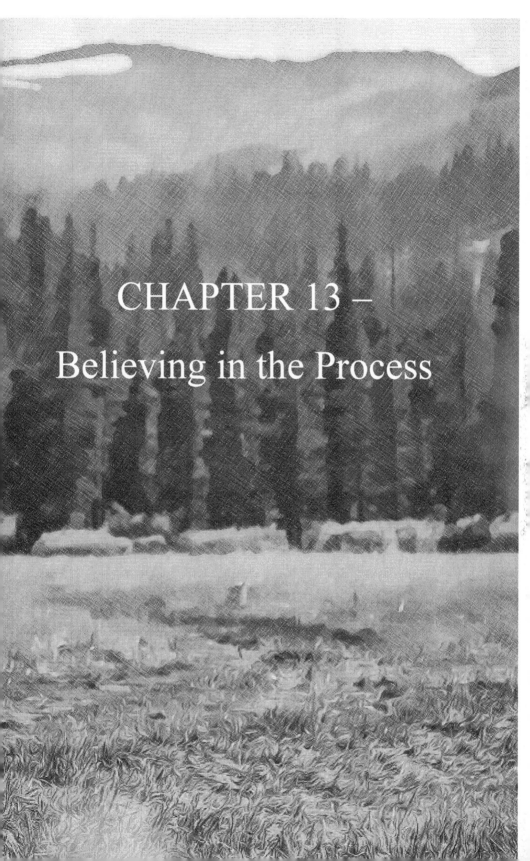

CHAPTER 13 –

Believing in the Process

As I stated on page 2 of this book, this is a simple program. If you can...

Live in the Mystery...
Show up,
Believe in the Process,
And let go of your Expectations...
...Magic becomes real,
And Dreams come true,
As Power, Passion and Possibility conspire to unleash your
High Performance Life.

Film and comedy legend Woody Allen once said, "Showing up is 80% of life." And while this simple act might seem self-explanatory, a lot of people choose not to show up in the first place. Convinced it won't matter anyway, they stay home. They don't make the call. They don't reach out.

When there are choices to be made, they make "no choice," and by doing that they cut themselves off from 100% of life's magical opportunities.

I am assuming that you are *not* one of these people, because you've already read this far. And if you are, I presume you'd like to be something different.

Here's step one: show up.

One of the barriers to "showing up," is the false belief that we're already out of the running. We're conditioned to the belief that the top 10% are always going to win, have all the money and get the best jobs.

Looking at the Forbes 1000 list of richest individuals doesn't do much to defeat the notion that a very small percentage of people actually do hold a vastly disproportionate amount of the world's wealth.

What if you're not competing with them?
What if you're not even competing with the other 90%?
What if the only person you're competing with is you?
Take a snapshot.
Where are you right now, at this precise moment?

Isn't it conceivable that you could be better tomorrow?
Just thinking that thought made you better than you were
already.

Growing up in Post-War America, the term "Made in Japan" meant inexpensive but inferior quality mass-produced goods. Meanwhile, the Japanese had determined that their pathway out of total defeat was to reinvent themselves and everything they did.

They adopted the term "Kaizen." The two characters used to express this idea are "Change" and "Good." Combining them creates the concept that "change *is* good."

□ □

Smart Japanese manufacturers began looking at every aspect of design, engineering and production. Instead of going for huge breakthroughs, they recognized and rewarded small but continuous improvements. And after only about 20 years they ended up with powerhouse brands like Honda, Sony and Nikon. Today, a Yamaha piano is held in as much reverence as a Steinway, and a Lexus automobile (built by Toyota) is totally competitive with a Mercedes-Benz or BMW.

The lesson here is you don't need to be where you intend to be right this minute, so be patient. But, also be persistent, because it's not going to happen overnight. Instead of giant leaps, it's going to take a lengthy series of small steps to get there.

Be patient, persistent, have faith,
And have a little fun along the way.

That's what we mean when we say, "believe in the process." It means you can have faith that the path you're on is the right one; that it will deliver to that destination you seek, even when (especially when) it does not feel like you're where you want to be at the present moment.

One of the ways I have learned to believe in my own "process" is to create a consistent start to my day. I had already spent enough time thinking about my "bad habits." I decided to flip the coin and concentrate on developing a series of "good habits." So, the first two things I added to my daily routine were fitness and reading.

I quickly realized if I began every day this way, I could arrive at a level of physical and intellectual energy that increased my effectiveness throughout the day. And I needed every edge I could get, because I was out there pioneering the new frontiers of technology, competing with a whole lot of people who were just as smart and determined as me.

I was running my third venture capital-backed start-up, Exit 41. Back then I was constantly in fundraising mode, always pushing the envelope in terms of how much cash we could raise, keep on hand, and use to fuel the operation.

Because there are a lot of great "startups", the strength of your business plan was what attracted the VC investment, and we had been successful in gaining commitments from investors on both coasts. Yet we were still skating on very thin ice, and on one particular Friday, we almost went through that ice.

Dial back to the preceding day, when I looked at our books and realized that I would not have the money to make payroll without another infusion of cash by precisely 3:00 PM the following afternoon.

Fortunately, our investors on both the East and West Coast had agreed they would put in the money. Convinced we were going to dodge another bullet, I went to bed. The following morning, I woke up at 4:30 AM to hit the gym, just like normal. Before I left I took the *abnormal* step of looking at my email, where I saw that the West Coast investors had decided to back out of the investment. My company would be insolvent in less than 12 hours.

This news was certainly not how I would have chosen to start my day. I could easily have panicked, but then it hit me: what could I do about it at that precise moment?

It was still the middle of the night in California, so a pleading email to the investors probably wouldn't be read, and even if it was, it would probably just be a source of irritation to the people I wanted to influence.

I decided instead to just go ahead with my daily routine. I pedaled the exercise bike. I read the Wall Street Journal, and another chapter in a book I was into at the moment. This wasn't an attempt to put my head in the sand and ignore the ticking time bomb that awaited my 60 employees later in the day. Instead it was to put myself in the space that I had already found to be so positive and productive for me.

I had a process. I believed in it and I stuck to it. And within a couple of hours, I felt really ready to take on whatever the day had in store for me, bankruptcy or not. By the time the sun came up on the West Coast it was late morning in Boston, and that bankruptcy clock just kept on ticking.

I got the investors on the phone and made one of the best pitches of my life, getting everyone back to the commitments we had all shared the day before, reminding them why we were here, and what we were capable of doing if we could just keep the development process going.

And by the time three o'clock rolled around, even though my company was just hours away from extinction, we pulled it out. The investors came through, and we lived to fight another day.

The way I approached that day made me a believer. First it helped me to believe that the rest of the day would play out properly because I didn't compromise on the things that gave me power every day. And it made me a believer that for me, this was the way to start every day.

What is the best way for you to start your day?

Look at your 168 Hour Life chart and make sure you're putting the right priorities in the right places.

Here comes another challenge:

Let go of your expectations.

This can be a tough one. We're taught to have expectations of ourselves from an early age. And our beliefs too, whatever form they may take, are usually formed while we were still in our parents' arms. Expectations and beliefs are both deep-seated in us, and we have to seriously contend with them if we want to live our version of THPL. In fact, this is where rubber hits the High Performance road.

The next challenge is letting go of all those expectations we've created for *ourselves*. First let's look at that previous sentence.

Question: Who created the expectations?

We did!

Sure, when we were kids we wanted to achieve good grades in school so we could rise to our parents' and teachers' expectations and earn their approval. Similarly, we wanted to live up to our bosses' expectations of us. And we wanted to *exceed* the expectations of those whose love and affection we sought. Fast forward to now:

Whose expectations are you living up to?

Of course, your family, friends and co-workers have a right to certain expectations of you, but that's not what we're talking about. We're talking about those expectations that we'll fail because we're not smart enough or tough enough, that we're somehow unworthy of success.

How much would you like to drop those like a hot rock?
What's stopping you?

How about changing our expectations to facilitate,
rather than limit, our success?
Here's what I know:

When you're living The High Performance Life,
it becomes impossible to have anything less than magical
expectations,
because you are in a constant state of creation,

in partnership with the rest of planet Earth and all its inhabitants.

I can't think of a more thrilling way to live. Letting go of expectations does not mean that we prance off down some dreamy path paved with idyllic outcomes. Life will continue to serve up its share of not-so-great realities with unpredictable dependability.

We need to be able to use both intuition and critical thinking effectively, both our heart and our head. Do the numbers add up? Great. Does it feel right? Yes or no?

In high risk situations, we certainly want to be sure that both tests are met. Using one to the exclusion of the other can be a recipe for disaster. That's why living The High Performance Life is such an advantage. It enables us to assemble a growing "tool box" of skills, enabling us to dream the best version of our own reality, then design and execute a plan to realize that dream.

Exercise – What Pushed Your Buttons?

Think back to the story about the Panama City Ironman. You're either left feeling inspired or you think Joe Gagnon is the craziest person alive, or some combination thereof.

In the space below (or in your THPL journal), write about what would you do in a similar situation?

_____

_____

What's the furthest you've ever "pushed the envelope?"

_____

_____

What's the one thing you've always wanted to do, but didn't – what held you back?

_____

_____

What would you do differently today?

_____

_____

CHAPTER 14 – Ready State: It's Showtime

Is this all starting to fall into place? You can now see that when you combine these life and learning skills together, you get the proverbial "whole" that is "greater than the sum of its parts."

You become capable of living like a warrior in a maximum state of readiness, without ever having to stress out about it. You see people like this every day. The most obvious are athletes, but also politicians and businesspeople who seem to have that innate ability to become more focused the more chaotic their surroundings become. But they're even closer to home than that. They're next to you in traffic or behind you in line at the supermarket. And now you get to be one of them.

Living in the ready state means you have clear principles as a foundation for how to behave, you're keenly interested in your surroundings without being distracted by the noise. It means you are comfortable being uncomfortable, so when life comes your way, you are entirely ready to take whatever action is necessary.

What you do is entirely up to you.

When you live in the ready state, you are able to create a distraction-free environment around yourself, able to tune out anything that's not relevant. You're able to see order inside of chaos, because your only focus is on what you need to do next.

Now, just because you're in that ready state it doesn't mean everything is always going to work out. Life is a contact sport. That's why *resiliency* is another prized characteristic of The High Performance Life.

It could mean taking a real punch to your ego, or just not getting upset at those people who keep bumping your behind with their shopping cart at the supermarket. Resiliency is also being able to work through all those circumstances without letting negative energy take you over.

Resiliency is the ability to recognize when it's time to change direction. This doesn't mean you're running away from a problem, far from it. It means that if you're on the side of a rock face and you realize there's a better way to get to your ultimate goal than the course you're on, you choose to go the better way. It's not a defeat. It's a course correction that takes you on the pathway to success.

And as you now know, all of these skills are cumulative. Each one builds on all the others, compounding your abilities. You are truly on the magical THPL journey already. Just look at how far you've come in this short time.

Imagine what's next!

Exercise – Just Say Yes

When you say "YES" to LIFE (invitations, opportunities, challenges) magic accelerates your life.

In order to strengthen your "THPL" magic muscles, pick one of the following challenges and say "YES" to it (meaning: do it!)

- Tell someone you love them
- Hug a stranger
- Tell someone they're attractive
- Tell someone your deepest fear
- Tell someone your proudest achievement
- Do the *Macarena*
- Do the Twist, Mashed Potato, or the Superman Hip Hop Dance Step in public
- Ask someone to teach you the *Macarena*, Twist, Mashed Potato, or the Superman Dance Step
- Yodel like you're in the Swiss Alps
- Do an Elvis Impersonation
- Walk like an Egyptian

- Put change in a stranger's parking meter
- Put a note on a neighbor's car that says, "You are loved more than you know" – take it the next level and *sign the note*

In the space below (or in your THPL Journal) write about your experience saying, "Yes!"

_____

_____

_____

_____

_____

PART IV –

FITNESS

PREFACE

Integrating physical and spiritual activity into our daily lives,
to Create a body, mind and soul that is both healthy and powerful.

In this section you will experience the following concepts:

The Physical & Spiritual Vessel

Accountability

Always Happy, Never Satisfied

Fulfillment

CHAPTER 15 –
The Physical and
Spiritual Vessel

The Physical Vessel

In my humble opinion, life's priorities go like this: I need to take care of myself and my connection to the Universe first. That way I can take care of my family, and then my work, in that order. It will come as no surprise to you that I value fitness as the third core element of The High Performance Life.

Fitness operates on two distinct planes, the first of which is physical.

A strong body is the foundation, upon which I build a strong mind and a strong life around me. I feed my body the nutrition it requires. I exercise. I rest. I push it. I focus on it every day, and try to coax it to do a little bit more than it did yesterday. And, I take excellent care of it, because it's going to be my home the whole time I'm alive here with all of you.

Take a moment and just praise your body for taking you this far. Whatever shape you're in, you are alive, and that's a pretty miraculous thing by itself. We both know you're able to read and reason, and you have the brain that runs your body to thank for that.

Of course, there may be things about your body that trouble you. How it looks. How it performs. How it feels right now. While a small portion of that isn't in your control, a great deal of it is. The part that *is* in your control is where we focus ourselves in The High Performance Life.

Your body is a *study in reinvention*. Every day you discard billions of old cells and generate billions of new ones. You are in a constant state of regeneration, making it that much more possible for you to steer that process in a good direction, instead of just sitting around and waiting for it to happen.

Still there is a natural process of aging, which we have been taught is inevitable. I don't believe that.

I know I'm going to die someday. That's inevitable.

I know I will get older until my final day. That too is inevitable.

What's <u>not</u> inevitable is that my joints have to stiffen, and my tendons grow brittle. What's <u>not</u> inevitable is that my muscles grow weak, or become displaced by fat.

Even if you're of advanced age and some of these conditions have already arisen, I can't stress enough how much you can still do to change it. You may not be able to return to your youth, but you can certainly be better than what you are right now. Think about that for a minute.

What could you do this very moment to begin improving your body?

I maintain that if everyone simply put in one hour of moderate daily exercise, our health would improve across the board. There is serious clinical evidence that even moderate exercise is a huge preventer of heart disease, hypertension, type-II diabetes and many other ailments.

And it's not just strength I'm seeking. I also want to retain my agility and flexibility. There are so many programs already out there that deal with one aspect of fitness. I want my personal fitness to accelerate the potential of *every* part of my being.

What good is strength without agility? What good is agility without a sharp mind to direct our actions and shape our attitudes?

Beyond exercise, diet plays an enormous role here as well. And this is another "sore subject" for me, because diets, *fad diets* in particular, create an illusion of good physical health and fitness without ever once getting to the true core of what creates it. And only a few of them deal seriously with the lifestyle changes that are required to lose *and* retain lower weight.

Diets can cause us to lose weight, but they cannot keep us from reverting back. There is an indisputable fact: if you burn more calories[15] than you consume, you will lose weight over time. That's why programs such as "The Biggest Loser" combine rigorous physical training, along with a food intake that provides only enough calories to get them through the day without being malnourished.

The Spiritual Vessel

As you can easily see, I value physical fitness as a core of The High Performance Life. No less important is my spiritual fitness. And while it is vital to me, I wish to restate that The High Performance Life is totally ecumenical.

I was raised as a Roman Catholic and I certainly believe in a lot of the churches' teachings about how we should live our lives. However, I do not endorse any religion or belief system, other than to say that some form of positively-focused spirituality is vital to this endeavor. The form it takes is entirely up to you.

---

[15] Calories are actually a measurement of energy. We have been conditioned to view them only as a measurement of how much fat they will produce inside us. That is determined by how much fat we burn

I will state that The High Performance Life has become *my* personal connection to the Universe, because it embodies everything I believe, think and know. And I believe I know this much: each and every one of us has a spirit that lives inside of us, and my goal is to do my utmost to see that I use that spirit to the benefit of as many others as I can.

Questions such as who gave this spirit to me and where I'll be after this life I leave up to each individual to figure out. All the rest I leave up to the Universe and my ability to dream. And because I have been living The High Performance Life, my ability to dream has increased exponentially.

That is because the Life, Learning and Fitness we achieve is not *additive*: 1+1+1=3.

Instead, it is *multiplicative*: 1+1+1=*Infinity*.

Here are three simple behaviors I use to improve my spiritual fitness:

I try to become a servant to life as often as I can.

I practice the art of humility,

in the knowledge that I am no better, or worse than anyone

else.

I feel and express gratitude for every gift I have been given.

Multidimensionality

Another way of looking at Life + Learning + Fitness is that they are *multidimensional.* When combined in their fullest force, we become capable of soaring way past any known concept of "normal."

A multidimensional view is about thinking more broadly than any one individual component. It's not any one of the elements (Life, Learning, Fitness). It's all of them together, each supporting the others in harmony.

Here's a more practical example. You might be a good programmer, or a decent writer, or a budding designer, or a deep thinker. Any one of them is certainly good. But when you combine them, you become Steve Jobs. He combined several abilities and interests to do things that were truly remarkable. "But I'm not Steve Jobs" you say? Why not?

Look at yourself.

You have certain skills and abilities.
How do you already combine them to produce the results
you want?
How could you enhance them to produce even better
results?

Multidimensional thinking allows us to take different perspectives and look for the best pathway through, which might not be the one we've always taken. For example, when Jobs insisted that the "mouse" be the driving force behind the user interface[16], it was a risky move that was deeply concerning to Apple's investors, but it ended up revolutionizing computing.

---

[16] This insistence brought about a near-rebellion by his design and engineering team who insisted that removing the "cursor keys" from the keyboard would be confusing for consumers and a commercial disaster.

New perspectives enable us to embrace the notion that innovation often happens only through *disruption*: change in structure, change in order, change in direction. Only by accepting the new structure, order, and direction can we truly take a new path.

In today's world of light-speed innovation, it makes more sense than ever to make your life into The High Performance Life.

Okay…Time To Meet Sally

Several years ago, my daughters introduced me to a girl named Sally. It sounded like such a nice, friendly name. They told me Sally wasn't like the other girls. In fact, she wasn't a "real" girl at all. As I found out, it was a nickname for a pushup challenge they were doing at school, called "The Sally Challenge."

It sounded innocuous enough to me, something college kids would dream up to do in dorm rooms. And I already did lots of pushups, so how tough could it be?

They cautioned me that it might not be as easy as I thought. It wasn't.

Here's how the "Sally Challenge" goes. There is a song by Moby, called "Flower." It's actually an old children's song.

One of the repeated lyrics is *"Bring Sally up, bring Sally down"* and during this lyric, you are to push "up" and then go back "down" and hold that position, where you will discover that there are *many more* lyrics before you are told to come back "up" again. You're literally holding the most stressful position of the pushup for most of the song, which by the way lasts for 3 minutes and 26 seconds.

Even though I considered myself to be in peak physical condition, I was only able to make it to 2 minutes and 5 seconds on my first try. I was shocked! I could scarcely get halfway through the song!

That night I wrote an email (should have been a text – LOL) to a half dozen of my buddies, informing them about "The Sally Challenge." These were some of the most accomplished athletes I knew, and *none* of them were able to do it. I'm sure there are some people in the world that could do this the first time, but I wasn't one of them, nor were any of those among this elite and very fit group of friends.

The "Sally Challenge" became a daily fixation of mine, and as it turned out, a widening group of friends online. Each day we emailed back and forth about how far we got, inching our way through the song.

A couple of things happened because of this.

First, the collegiality of the conversation made my few seconds of daily improvement that much less mundane and boring. This "community" of individuals who were all going after the same goal helped share the load.

Second, that was the birth of my daily blog, posted like clockwork at 3:00 AM Eastern Time US, now for more than 1,600 continuous days.

And by the way, it took me more than a month to finally complete the "Sally Challenge."

Now it's your turn.

Exercise – The Sally Challenge

Purchase or download the song "Flower," by Moby[17] at https://itunes.apple.com/us/artist/moby/id789023 or on YouTube.

It might help to listen to the song once before trying the challenge, so you will get a full understanding of what you're doing, before you do it (that would be the "planning" it part before you "practice" it).

For "The Full Monty" version, you should begin the challenge in a military-style, face-down prone position, ready to perform the first push-up.

Begin the song.

---

[17] Please use only pay to play sites and *do not download a bootleg version.* I'm sure you understand by now how that would go against the integrity of The High Performance Life.

At the first mention of "Bring Sally Up, Bring Sally Down," you perform a single up/down pushup and come to rest in the "down" position with your arms flexed and your chest not touching the floor. Continue this activity with every mention of "Bring Sally Up, Bring Sally Down" for as long as you can.

If you are unable to do military-style push-ups you can vary this challenge in a number of ways:

- Plank push-ups, where you rest on your elbows instead of your hands, lowering the distance between you and the floor.
- Knee push-ups where you rest your knees instead of your toes on the floor, creating a shorter fulcrum.
- Wall push-ups, where you stand against a wall or doorframe and lean into the "stressed" position.

In any of these variants, it is important to use an activity that is *not easy* for you. If you are able to finish the entire song the first time you try it, you have set your sights too low. The point is that you want it to be hard enough that you are *not* able to finish Sally the first time you try.

Be mindful of your desire to *quit* for all of the "right" reasons:

- Pain/Discomfort
- Fatigue
- The feeling like "this is stupid"

Face these challenges down and overrule them.

Additionally, go back and review your "Breakthrough Goal" from the exercise in Chapter 5. Plant this goal in your mind as you do the Sally Challenge.

Make this a daily part of your "168 Hour Life."

Watch and note your improvement.

Apply this same energy and focus to your THPL Breakthrough Goal – then the rest of your life.

If you can do "Sally" you can do anything.

CHAPTER 16 –
Accountability –
THPL Community

By now it's clear that surrounding ourselves with a likeminded, mutually-inspiring community can have tremendous benefits, as demonstrated by the popularity of churches, clubs, committees, sports teams, gatherings of all types.

Human beings are hard-wired for connectivity to one another: we've been operating as "packs" for tens of thousands of years. When we work together, we achieve greater individual and collective goals.

On The High Performance Life journey, we are all in pursuit of stronger bodies and stronger minds, but still there remain emotional challenges that can be difficult, if not impossible, to bear alone.

And why should we?

Many famous songs have been written and recorded about this connection we share, Dionne Warwick's *"That's What Friends Are For,"* The Hollies' *"He Ain't Heavy, He's My Brother,"* and Natalie Merchant's *"Trouble Me"* are a few that immediately come to mind. The benefits of having a like-minded community reduces our fear of being alone, strengthens our resolve, gives us more leverage toward manifesting our goals, along with positive peer pressure to keep us going, stretching, and developing our own unique version of The High Performance Life.

On the High Performance Life journey we now hold ourselves accountable for higher, better, more focused results. We have let go of past regrets, so that we can see anew, with fresh eyes, the road ahead.

Instead of blaming others for our deficits, we ask ourselves

What can I do differently?
How can I help this situation get better?

A High Performance Life community around us validates these actions and helps cement them into a mutual "to do" culture that brings everyone to a higher plane of existence.

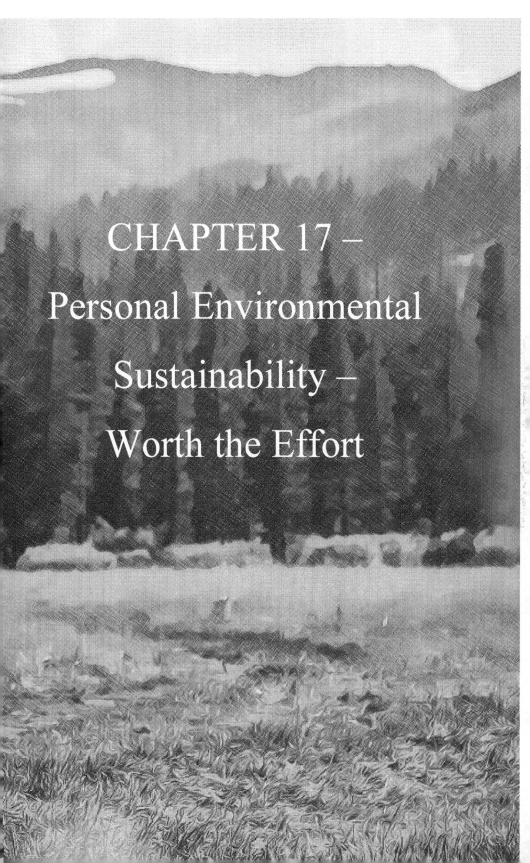

CHAPTER 17 –

Personal Environmental

Sustainability –

Worth the Effort

There Is Always Something You Can Do

You don't get four million air miles without spending a good amount of time in airports. They are confounding places at best, and ever since the TSA rules went into place over ten years ago, the utility value of my reusable Nalgene bottle has sadly been diminished.

So, what is a boy (or girl) to do?

I don't like buying water in plastic bottles, but I found myself on an otherwise utterly forgettable trip through yet another airport debating the merits of buying a ridiculously overpriced bottle of water from the terminal convenience store. Yes, I knew these bottles will be on the planet for 500+ years, and yes, I knew we need to reduce usage as quickly as we can.

But air travel is a very dehydrating experience, and so I took the big step, paid way too much for the water, and drank it in a few big swigs. Now what? I searched for a recycling bin. None in sight. Ugh!

How frustrating. Keep looking? Not likely as I had just a few minutes until my plane would be boarding. What would you do?

What's the big deal? What's one more bottle? Who would notice? No one was looking. Ah, but Mother Earth is always watching. I thought about the 50 billion bottles used a year in the US alone.

Then I thought about the Texas-sized island of floating discarded plastic, trapped by swirling currents in the middle of the Pacific Ocean. I thought about the 1,000,000 seabirds and 100,000 sea mammals who die from plastic ingestion each year.

I thought about the billions of fish who are found with toxic plastic in their digestive tracts, and how that all non-biodegradable trash works its way up the food chain into the fish we consume.

I thought about the fact that only 23% of all discarded plastic is recycled and the fact that I could either become another small part of this gigantic problem, or I could become a small part of its solution. I thought about my THPL path, and what it had taught me about taking responsibility for my actions.

And then came the clincher. I thought about my daughters when they were young, and how much pride they took in sorting the recycling and bringing it to the curb each week. I thought about the young people I mentor in CHIME IN (The Change Is Me International) and how they look up to me as a role model. And then I determined to do my personal best to make sure that *one less bottle* would find its way to a landfill.

I sheepishly smiled to myself and stuffed the empty bottle in my backpack to take it home to be recycled, an action so small as to be almost insignificant when you put it up against the global challenges we face.

But when I sat down in my seat on the plane, I felt better about the day, and better about me. This seemingly small action gave me a momentary feeling that I was contributing to a more sustainable life and a more sustainable planet. I felt so good, I was able to actually catch a little much needed shuteye on that flight home. Sustainability. That has to be integral to The High Performance Life.

But what is "sustainability?" I mean it's one of those "pop-concept buzzwords" that people love to bandy about, like "natural" and "organic." And as you probably know, a lot of that is "just talk," designed by marketers to get us to buy a certain product. But what is sustainability really, and how does it fit into your THPL journey?

In my definition, sustainability means simply that we must act in a way that supports our planet. As we build stronger minds, bodies, and souls, we must give to our planet as much as we take from it, if not more, because it's the only home we'll ever have (despite all the excitement about people going to Mars).

In the same way that THPL requires that we focus on a fulfilled life it also asks that we live *mindfully* on the earth. And if we are to do this, we need to live *sustainably*.

On our THPL journey, the air we breathe, the food we eat, all of it is utterly dependent on Mother Earth. We rely on her for everything from animals to insects, from plants to trees, from to air to water. In fact, all that is around us is vital to our ability to live The High Performance Life.

But, does recycling one plastic bottle make a difference?

Is recycling what sustainability is about? Absolutely. But it's only one factor in an overall sustainability. While recycling one bottle is indeed a small act, it is symbolic of a shift in attitude, a focus on living a sustainable life, one that's in harmony with the world around us.

So yes, I need to recycle and I need to spread the word about it.

And there is no time like the present to get started on our sustainability journey. We can start with big steps or small steps. In fact, living THPL by its very definition means you are taking responsibility for looking at your life through an environmental lens.

For example, think about what you consume, the things you buy, eat, and use for transportation. Think about what you produce, and what you throw away.

We all have lots of little daily habits. Some of those habits we might be more aware of than others. But, each day we make choices about how we live on our planet. Part of a sustainable THPL is moving from unconscious habits to conscious choices on what we consume and what we create. It matters and it matters a lot!

As I dozed in and out of sleep on that airplane, I contemplated how we can take these big ideas and make them actionable. What would be a simple structure for me and others who are on our THPL journey to embrace and use?

What if we all worked together to stop the unsustainable behaviors? That's a worthy dream to plug into the "Dream It" phase of a shared Sustainable THPL.

What if we all started making lots of little choices, which lead to bigger and better things for Mother Earth and our fellow humans? How about we start with a self-assessment? What are you doing right now that you could change or improve on your THPL path toward living a sustainable life? What can you point to that you already do? Surely, you already have some good habits you've acquired that are good for the planet (you wouldn't be attracted to this book were it not so!)

Exercise – Your Sustainable Life

List as many things as you can think of that you already do in relation to sustainability. You might be pleasantly surprised by the path you are on.

_____

_____

_____

Now list as many things you could change, do differently, do better, to live a <u>more</u> sustainable life? How can you plug these actions into your 168 Hour Week?

_____

_____

_____

_____

Sustaining Sustainability – It's Easier than You Think

"Never doubt that a small group of thoughtful, committed citizens can change the world, indeed, it's the only thing that ever has." – **Margaret Mead**

Part of what makes it challenging to live sustainably is that many of the concepts surrounding it can often seem a bit "obtuse" and hard to connect to our personal lives. We hear about our "carbon footprint." But what is that? It's hard to get aligned to things that are difficult to understand.

Working our goals within the realms of Life, Learning and Fitness, we seek to manifest things that we can touch and feel, that are intuitive and easy to embrace. So, as we think about sustainability there are some simple changes that we can make that can bring about a bigger impact. And we want them to be the ones that matter to each of us individually.

There is a learning curve involved in the sustainable THPL. And there isn't one specific formula to follow. Where you live, be it urban or rural, whether you travel a lot or stay close to home, so many variables impact the look and feeling of your personal sustainable THPL existence. But the truth is, *small actions matter*. When no one is looking, it matters. All of us pitching in makes a difference. There are countless opportunities to do that.

For example, in our home, we can remember to turn off the lights or change to ultra-low consumption LED fixtures. We can recycle, or try composting. If we're more ambitious, we can think about how we can add high-efficiency appliances, windows and doors. If we're really ambitious, we can invest in solar panels and reduce our dependence on the electrical grid. There are many ways that we can make a positive impact; we just need to embrace the one's that we feel most strongly about and then go after them. And if we are lacking in ideas, they are only a mouse click or a conversation away.

For starters, there are numerous "footprint" calculators online that give you a sense of your current impact on the earth. Look one or two up (you can try "carbon footprint" or "ecological footprint") and see where you land.

Since I travel so much, one of my biggest actions has been to always strive to use less stuff. It simplifies the packing process and makes me lighter on my feet, but it also means I'm consuming less raw material, less packaging, and spending less on things that I have discovered I can really quite easily do without. I know we live in a consumer-driven economy, so reducing consumption might seem heretical to some. But what if we focused the dollars we invest on "stuff" in tools and technologies that enable us to live more sustainably. I'm sure the economics will balance out, and the long-term effects of this approach can't help but improve our planet's overall health.

As using less has become a habit, I find it actually makes my life easier. Just like other sustainability habits can save you money, get you healthier, and support your community, some practices just plainly help to simplify your life. You'll see on the next page a chart of possible practices. This is just a sampling but I hope it will give you some ideas to research, to plan and to put into practice as you move your personal version of The High Performance Life in a more sustainable direction.

A "Sustainability Sampler"

	Food	Transportation	Purchasing	House	Other
Novice	Carry a reusable mug/ water bottle. Avoid the "dirty dozen" - most heavily sprayed crops - buy organic. Avoid consuming endangered fish. Reduce consumption of meat, especially the "factory-produced" variety	Don't idle your car unnecessarily. Carpool. Purchase a vehicle with the highest possible EPA mileage.	Bring reusable bags for shopping. Buy media (books, music, etc.) digitally. Use eco-friendly, and fewer, personal hygiene products. Choose products with less packaging.	Turn off/unplug electronics when not in use. Do some simple weatherizing. Start recycling and produce less garbage.	Enjoy the outdoors! Use daylight for your work instead of turning the lights on. Take shorter showers and re-use those towels at the hotel.
Intermediate	Get more food grown locally - CSA, farmer's market. Set up a worm compost bin in your house or a compost pile in your yard. Participate in a "cow-share" or "dairy share".	Walk or bike more often to work or for errands. Use it for fitness! Monitor your carbon footprint - try to lower it each year. Participate in a car-sharing program.	Buy Fair Trade. Share instead of buy (like a lawnmower). Search out and support B Corporations	Responsibly recycle batteries, electronics, motor oil and lightbulbs. Choose low-use (energy, water) appliances. Use only green-cleaning products.	Contribute to conservation/ restoration efforts with $$ or time. Avoid toxins for pests - research eco-friendly alternatives. Hang your clothes to dry.
Advanced	Participate in a community garden, or build your own. Consume at least 80% of your food from the first 3 food shed zones (see image)	Go totally car-less. Purchase carbon credits/offsets anytime you use fossil-fueled public transport (like flying)	Use a service like "Freecycle" to give/get things you need. Buy less - and always organic, or recycled content, or produced with renewable energy, etc.	Recycle/compost everything you can. Aim for zero waste to landfill. Retrofit your house to be net positive energy with renewables (solar panels, for example)	Calculate, and stay within, your own water footprint. Do a chemical inventory of your house/life and substitute out all toxins.

In the following pages we'll get more into nutrition. For now, grab a glass of water, choose something that is not packaged, eat more fruits and vegetables, look for super foods like kale, broccoli, blueberries, avocados, and make sure to increase your protein and fat intake. Most of all, don't eat as an activity. It is these little decisions that make for a better THPL journey.

On your sustainable THPL journey, you can be guided by a few principles:

- Minimize waste to landfill
- Shrink your carbon footprint
- Always think about using less stuff
- Reduce/eliminate your use of toxins
- Appreciate/support the natural world
- Share about the ways you are living a more sustainable life with friends. Sharing is a key part of the journey.

When you spend more time on your THPL journey you will find that you get attached and connected to many things. For example, there are the beautiful trails to run, glorious mountains to hike, breathtaking vistas to see, multicolored sunsets that dazzle, magical snowflakes to be enchanted by, and so much more. And there are times when we are on our journey that we can take for granted the splendor and beauty of all that surrounds us. We must stay vigilant and aware of that which we love. Our call, then is to put effort into protecting Mother Earth; to treat her like another living being, the host of all that we do. If we can live this way, the outcome will be more blessings than we can fathom for us and all life on the planet.

Exercise – Sustainability

What about the sustainable life speaks to you the most? What things do you want to learn more about?

_____

_____

List your top 2 to 3 strategies for each of the following questions:

What will you do to reduce your garbage?

_____

_____

_____

What will you do to reduce your carbon footprint?

_____

_____

What will you do to reduce the toxins in your life?

_____

_____

What can you share rather than buy?

_____

_____

What other actions can you take to be more sustainable in THPL?

_____

_____

CHAPTER 18 –

Nutrition…Ugh

For many people, the mere mention of the word "nutrition" can cause them to lose their appetite. And if you only look at it from a clinical or academic point of view, the subject of nutrition can be dry and confusing.

But by now I think you know me well enough to guess that we *aren't* going down that path. As you embark on your THPL journey, I encourage you to begin thinking about food and nutrition in an exciting and multi-dimensional way. And to do that, I invite you to take yet one more stroll down "Joe's Memory Lane."

I am one of those lucky people who had a grandmother who lived with us for many years. Having that multi-generational influence in my life was utterly normal for me growing up, but I now realize what a blessing it was; one I feel is less and less available to many families these days. And this wasn't just *any* grandma: mine was a "Nona," an *Italian* grandmother.

Like many Italian grandmothers, mine loved to cook. And she cooked *real* food, from scratch, with fresh natural ingredients from a recipe book she stored in her head, instead of an iPad. I can still remember her homemade pasta on Mondays, delicious soups on Tuesdays, and sumptuous Sunday dinners where she pulled out all the stops and we all sat around the table, celebrating our well-being, and the fact that we were a family who loved one another very much.

No matter how simple the recipe, every meal my Nona cooked was a flavor festival, transforming our house into a bouquet of tantalizing aromas during the entire process. To this day, if I catch the scent of basil or tomato sauce, I am instantly transported back to our Yonkers house, and my salivary glands are turned on in anticipation. Sense memories are so powerful.

Do you have a food memories like that? Where eating was an experience, not just a necessary activity. Where food nourished your soul as well as your body. Good, real food, rather than something you mindlessly stuff in your mouth on the way to somewhere "more important"?

It seems to me that in much of our fast-paced world we've lost the culture of food, the goodness of food, the quality of food prepared every day from fresh ingredients with no "additives", except for the occasional sprinkle of hot pepper. There I go, down memory lane once again!

Except for these powerful sense memories, we can't go back in time. But we can build from these special moments and remember how to make eating fun, nutritious, and good for our overall performance. The more we bring conscious thought to the food we eat, the better the results for our body and mind. After all, food is fuel and as we push our performance curve, the fuel we add to our bodies becomes more and more critical to success.

Consider that food not only fuels your body along your THPL journey, it is a cultural part of life.

Exercise – Defining Food

Take a moment to reflect on what "real food" means to you.
Take a walk down your own "memory lane," and
contemplate a "meal memory" that gave you both great
pleasure and nutrition. Describe it in the space below:

_____

_____

_____

_____

_____

_____

_____

_____

_____

Food Matters

The first time I realized that food mattered was years ago when a co-worker of mine told me she was starting a diet business. I winced at first, as I hate "diets" as a rule. And did the world really need one *more* diet? But as she began explaining it to me, my skepticism faded away. Hers was a very simple formula that has stuck with me ever since.

The core principle was that we eat an average of 21 meals a week. And that we need to make sure that 16-17 of those meals would fit a good food profile: high in nutrition, balanced in content, and modest in volume. For the other 4-5 meals, we could indulge ourselves a bit, have some fun, eat a bit more, enjoy some less nutrient dense foods (like pizza and chips) and still allow ourselves to feel good about eating it.

Of course, we can also eat 21 "great" meals if we choose, the point is that we do not need to be "perfect" or "stress" over every meal.

Her perspective, with which I wholeheartedly agree, is that if we are "directionally correct" more often than not, then we are headed in the right direction.

We need to take time to enjoy good food…to become aware of what constitutes good food…and to experience the connections between what we eat and the other elements of THPL.

Exercise – Your Food Week
(Part 1)

Think about your 21 meals this past week. How many of them were "good" for you? How many were "not so good"? In the space below, describe what could you have changed to get more into balance?

_____

_____

_____

_____

_____

_____

_____

Enjoyment, Awareness, and Interconnectedness

Do you remember what you had for lunch yesterday? It becomes easier to eat junk food when eating is just a passing activity. *Enjoying* food happens best when you add a dose of awareness to it. In other words, pay attention to when you may be satisfying your taste buds or eating for emotional reasons. In fact, as many "food tech" companies know, our bodies tend to be hardwired to crave fat and sugar. And at the same time our bodies do well with a nice balance between protein, fat and sugar. The smartest thing we can do, when it comes to food, is to contemplate the outcomes we want to create, and then we can align how we eat to meet those objectives.

Exercise – Your Food Week
(Part 2)

Take about 3 to 5 days to keep a food journal, writing down everything you eat and drink. Become aware of what you put in your body. Identify what energized you and what depleted you.

_____

_____

_____

_____

_____

_____

_____

_____

Growing Food Awareness

The other side of food awareness is knowing more about what is healthy, what will make you feel good in your body and what will give you sustained energy. There are a lot of food "fads" out there, and much of it is filled with contradictory advice. Meat/no meat. Milk/milk substitutes. Carbs/no carbs. Nutritional advice can get really confusing, and a whole lot of people are making a lot of money peddling their version of what a "good diet" looks like.

Where diet is concerned, I am not here to peddle anything in particular. Instead, I will simply tell you what I've chosen to do, and you will discover for yourself what works best.

I decided some time ago to be vegetarian. I have found that a plant-based diet is easier to digest, fuels me better, and generally has less impact on the planet. Because I travel so much, this can be something of a challenge. However, I manage my eating by bringing some of my favorite food bars with me, stopping in the right places to get food when it is available and avoiding those food items that I would not eat otherwise. I also avoid processed foods and eat organic produce, despite its premium price. Very few of us know where the food on our table came from, how it was grown, handled, how far it traveled to get to us. Again, to the extent possible, I try to buy locally-grown foods. The industrial food complex has convinced us that we should have ripe strawberries available to us in the middle of December. In reality, those strawberries had to be grown in Chile and were picked long before they were ripe, so they could be shipped thousands of miles and arrive at what we've been taught is optimal "ripeness" when they hit the refrigerator case at your local supermarket. Having said that, I'm enough of a realist to recognize that fresh organic food is not as readily available in all parts of the country, so here are a handful of general principles you can follow:

- The less packaging the better. In other words, shop the outside aisles in your grocery store, and avoid the "brand-name" packaged produce.

- If you have to purchase packaged foods, *read the label*. If there are things you can't pronounce, it's probably something you want to avoid. Also count the number of ingredients in the package. Less than seven is great, more than 15 and you start to wonder, get close to 25 and you should run for the hills (other than a chemical experiment what could take 25 ingredients to make?)

- Add color to your plate - dark greens, orange, red, yellow, blue, purple - this means exploring the diversity of vegetables –the more seasonal and vibrant the better for you!

- Become familiar with superfoods to have on hand as snacks.

- If you can, know where your food comes from. Know your farmer. Buy food from a CSA (Community Supported Agriculture) group, or a local farmer's market.

One way to improve our internal workings relates to antioxidants and their proper consumption on a regular basis. Antioxidants are one of the hot concepts in the health food world these days.

You can spend a lot of money at the store loading up on vitamins and supplements that boast a high antioxidant content, or you can just eat some great natural foods and drinks that contain the right amounts of truly natural antioxidants.

Some examples include, spinach, quinoa, kale, acai, goji berries, red wine, dark chocolate, walnuts, almonds, cacao, broccoli (my favorite), and berries all of which are amazing for you. In addition, you can explore and research other "newer" antioxidant rich foods and have some fun discovering what can really help you achieve your best version of THPL. Chia seeds (remember these), artichoke hearts, black tea and turmeric are examples of some other non-traditional antioxidant rich foods.

Have fun exploring!

Food as Fuel for the Athlete

I can remember as if it was yesterday when a friend told me how to think about a triathlon. He said you swim to get to the bike, you bike to get to the run, and you eat to get to the finish. This mantra has stuck with me since then and while I would love to say that I am perfect in following his advice I am not. For all that we train, all that we study and learn about techniques that will improve our performance, even endurance athletes still do not get this perfect. And when we do not get it right, we can pay a dear price.

It is a game of trial and error and for an ultra-athlete, long-distance triathlete or a mountaineer, you learn quickly that your nutrition plan is as critical as the gear you bring. All of your planning, training, and execution can get compromised without proper nutrition. While intellectually it makes sense to eat properly, to eat at the right intervals, and to stay hydrated and "topped off" with calories, there are times that without a proper plan (and reminders), you can put yourself at risk and make the challenge even harder. One way to address the issue is to adopt rules before you start, such as

"I am going to eat every XX hours, or I will eat XX kinds of foods."

It is worth practicing before you go on an epic adventure. The more your body gets use to the "right" kinds of nutrition, at the right time, the better off your THPL journey will be.

And Then There's the "Oreo" Effect

What you find out quickly on long runs, races, rides, and hikes is that your body consumes an average of 500-800 calories an hour. Short yourself on calories and the day will get very hard or it will simply end before you want it to[18].

The other thing you learn is that your palate, your gut, and even your sensibility can all seem to conspire against you. What you craved an hour ago, you can't stomach now. For a while you could chew food and now you can only drink calories. And the crazy thing about it is this can change at

---

[18] See DNF on page 27

each race. What worked last time might not work this time. So, it's really important to discover what can reliably work for you, because there are no shops that you can stop at during an Ironman.

I know this may come as a big surprise to many of you, but, I've discovered that *Oreos* are great, just about all the time. I know. I just finished telling you about my pristine dietary habits and here I am endorsing one of the most popular "junk foods" on the planet. It all comes back to that intense caloric need we create when we are exercising our body to its maximum. There is something about that cookie that just makes me want to eat more than one and when I need calories amazingly they can get me to the finish line.

Without pushing too much "science" around, it is important to note and to understand that one of the reasons the "Oreo fix" works so well is that as we move into a state of high aerobic activity it is easier for the body to quickly metabolize sugars (carbohydrates) and turn them into energy. As we go longer and harder, our nervous system starts "screaming" for glucose (sugar) to keep stimulating our muscles. And this process works even better when something tastes good. We get a multi-leveled good feeling, both taste and outcome.

With simple sugars consumed *while* exercising, performance remains stable and we can go for longer periods of time at optimal levels of performance. This "eat while exercising" should be done when we are out for more than two hours. It really is not recommended to carry these eating behaviors into inactive parts of our life. It is important to understand that when our bodies are in "normal" mode, we have enough sugar and fat stored in them to keep us going for a long period of time.

Binging on sugar when we are not exercising is not only unnecessary but can bring on other potentially negative effects, as the fact that Type-II Diabetes is a national epidemic would seem to indicate. The key to all of this is to be aware that there is a direct link between activity and energy requirements. We just need to think before we eat and be smart about the way to do that. When this happens, performance improves in all aspects of our lives and life is good. Very good.

I hope I have shown you that what works in an "event" does not work for everyday so, please do keep your "Oreo habit" to a manageable amount.

And then when you're back to your day to day life, having discipline about what you eat is maybe one of the most important elements to your High Performance Life.

Think about it, we are supposed to decide what we eat, how much, how healthy etc. But in our "super busy" lives we often opt for "quick" versus "good." We eat out, we let others choose, we buy packaged foods where someone else decided what goes in them, and often just for the sake of being able to package the food in the first place, I believe that what we really need to develop is food discipline. We would not compromise big decisions in other parts of our life would we? Think about it, if you're stuck in traffic do you decide to drive up the median? If you need money do you go out and rob a bank? Of course not! We do the sensible thing. We follow rules and obey laws, because they are there for our well-being. We need to develop the same attitude toward food.

You don't need to follow some prescribed "program" or special diet. You just need to slow down and think, then eat.

What you eat should be up to you and it should fit your lifestyle, nutritional needs, and performance requirements. When we do this, and take agency over the way we eat all good things happen. Have fun!

Exercise – Your Food Week (Part 3)

List 3-5 things you want to know more about and will research (for example: superfoods, local CSAs …). Then, list 3 - 5 habits you plan to develop in relation to eating.

_____

_____

_____

_____

_____

_____

_____

_____

_____

Food(s) I Love

I have been a devoted amateur cook for quite some time. Studying food, tasting it, reading about it, and of course learning from experience. It is fun to be able to cook food that looks good, tastes good and has a great nutritional profile. Simple is as powerful as any approach and it starts with quality ingredients. It is hard to make food taste good if we compromise on what we use to make our meals. A few recipes that I find work for just about anyone are the following:

Simple Roasted Broccoli

One head of broccoli, chopped
4 whole cloves of peeled garlic
1T salt
1 t black pepper
2 T olive oil

Combine all ingredients, blend and turn out onto a 13x9 baking sheet

Roast broccoli in the oven for 35 minutes at 400 degrees

Baked Spinach Frittata

2 tablespoons extra-virgin olive oil
1 small onion chopped
1 package baby spinach
Kosher salt and freshly ground pepper
8 large eggs
½ C whole milk
4 tablespoons bread crumbs
1/2 cup crumbled feta cheese

Heat 2 tablespoons olive oil in a medium nonstick ovenproof skillet over medium-high heat. Add the onions and spinach and cook, stirring, until wilted, about 4 minutes. Stir in 1/2 teaspoon salt, and pepper to taste; remove from the heat. Whisk the eggs, 2 tablespoons breadcrumbs, milk and 1/2 teaspoon salt in a large bowl. Add the egg mixture and feta to the skillet and stir to combine. Sprinkle with the remaining 2 tablespoons breadcrumbs. Transfer the skillet to the oven and bake at 425 degrees until the frittata is set and the top is golden, or about 15-20 minutes.

Exercise – THPL Community Part Infinity

Make yourself a part of THPL Community through the following ways -

- Sign up to receive THPL daily blog:
- Follow THPL on Social media:
- Facebook:
  https://www.facebook.com/TheHighPerformance
  Life/
- Instagram:
  https://www.instagram.com/thehighperformanceli
  fe
- Twitter: https://twitter.com/THPLife

Create a THPL Community Group, using this book as your guide – share challenges and celebrate successes.

If you'd like support creating your own THPL LIVE weekly workshop, contact us to help you get started:

Joe@TheHighPerformanceLife.net

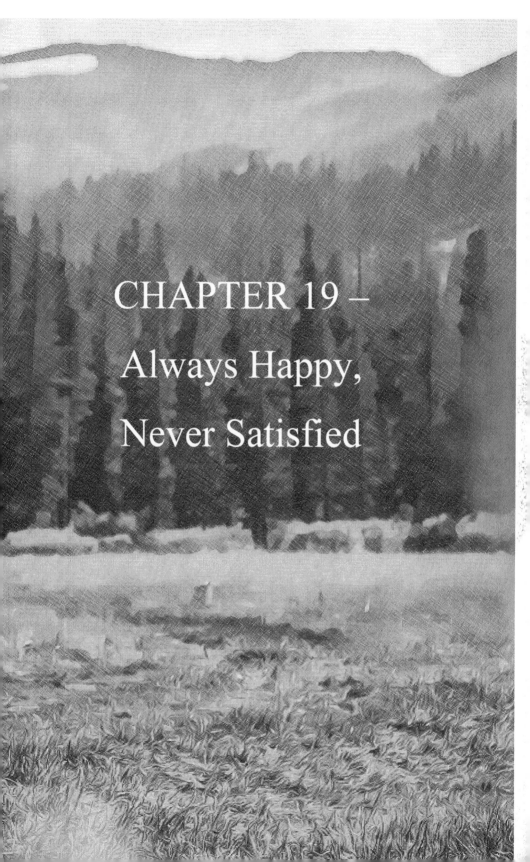

CHAPTER 19 –
Always Happy,
Never Satisfied

"Always happy, never satisfied." A skeptic might look at those words negatively. But that's what skeptics do, isn't it? I've moved *far* beyond skepticism.

To me, always happy, never satisfied, means that I can go to bed every night, completely spent and ready for sleep, with the knowledge that I did my best that day.

But it also brings the acceptance that I'm human and I didn't do everything perfectly. If I fell short, I know where it was, and can make a plan to fix it. And if I really fell short, causing disappointment in myself or others, I make a solemn plan to make it right, and do much better in the future. I don't just say "I'm sorry" and move on. I try to make sure that I never have to say, "I'm sorry" for the same thing twice.

Always happy, never satisfied is my way of saying to myself,

Yes, I'm 100% human. I will mess up.
Hopefully I will mess up less tomorrow than I did today.

And I will honor myself by feeling great about me, all of the time.

If you have already made these realizations, I'm glad to be a part of the human race alongside you. And if you're just now coming to them, welcome to the liberation of knowing that you're "one of us," and we accept you as you are.

Heck, *I'm* proud of you just for getting this far in the book! I tried my best to make it as brief and readable as possible, and hope you're finding meaning and purpose in it all.

And on the off-chance that you *have* found meaning and purpose in these pages that shows you a new direction your life might take, pat yourself on the back. Think of all you have to be proud of!

Now get over it!
Complacency isn't in your vocabulary anymore.
Ha!

Oh yes, there's always room in THPL for a little levity and humor (sometimes a lot!)

As you pursue The High Performance Life, you are now migrating from needs and wants to solutions and outcomes.

One final activity for you. Go back to your THPL Breakthrough Goal (from the bottom of chapter 5) and consider how you're doing with it. Ask yourself:

Can I improve it? Have I accomplished it? If not, why? And what will I do to get back on the horse? If so, what's next?

Fulfillment – What Do These Words Mean to You *Now*?

If you can *live in The Mystery*...

Show up,
Believe in the Process,
And let go of your Expectations...
...Magic becomes real,
And Dreams come true,
As Power, Passion and Possibility conspire to unleash your
High Performance Life.

CHAPTER 20 –
Run Joe, Run!

It's April 12th, 2017 and as I walk up to Border Control I'm already anticipating the quizzical looks and queries that have become commonplace on this adventure. "Sir, how long will you be in South Africa?" With my characteristic big grin, I reply, "I will be leaving this evening, so about 12 hours." The wheels in his head immediately start spinning, "Why such a short visit?"

I'm already wondering if he thinks I'm an international drug smuggler, so I put on my most earnest, non-criminal-looking face and offer my explanation. "I am on a journey to run six marathons, on six continents on six consecutive days."

He shrugs his shoulders, shakes his head, probably thinking, "Oh, so he's <u>not</u> a criminal. He's just crazy." He stamps my passport, and hands it back to me with a look of parental concern.

Then off I head to the next 26.2 mile run flowing in a rhythm that was now starting to become familiar. 12 to 14 hours of travel, 10 to 12 hours in country visiting and running. Wash, rinse, repeat. Today it's South Africa, and I'm halfway into a week that would eventually tally 37,500 miles and 59 hours of flying, 157 miles / 24 hours of running, a mere 13 hours of sleep, six continents, six days, hundreds of supporters and a constant state of motion. So, how did I find myself in this situation?

There are very few people who get to go to the moon, and we generally accept that as "just the way it is." And so, we don't do any preparation to leave Earth's safe and constant gravity. We don't condition ourselves, or learn new skills and techniques that will help us survive in an environment with no air. Because we're not ever going to the moon, right?

A lot of us, including me, create a similar way of thinking about what is possible for us. We stop ourselves from dreaming and doing remarkable things because we have little context for believing "big things" are possible. We think, "That's for them. I can't do that." And from that assumption we begin gathering all the evidence we need to build a solid case for why it will not happen. And that is right where we leave it, which is *nowhere*.

We limit how our lives evolve, constrain the journey that we are on, and settle for less than we are capable of. But hold on. If you've already read this far, I'm pretty sure that by now you have been coaxed, cajoled, and guided that such thinking is entirely dispensable! You now know that you can *Dream, Plan*, and *Practice* to *Do* almost anything you set your mind to.

I have come to realize that "Dreaming" and "Doing" are the bookends for how I want to live my life. "Planning" and "Practicing" are everything else. Over and over again, I have found the dreams I create really do come true, and so I just keep dreaming bigger, more improbable things and running six marathons on six continents in six days certainly ranks as one of the most fantastic things I've ever dreamt up.

Throughout my life, a whole lot of reasonable and well-intentioned people have challenged my thinking, my actions, and my way of living. They tell me I need to rest, that I shouldn't go there, that's dangerous. Sometimes they tell me "that's crazy," but I am compelled by this feeling that I'm going to be here for such a short time. Why would I not want to use this amazing resource that I've been blessed with to its fullest possible potential? I've never been one of those people who "plays to the middle." To me that axiom "everything in moderation" is the end of possibility.

And so, during a particularly long run in April of 2016, that familiar feeling started bubbling inside me once again. I needed a big challenge. Something beyond anything I had done. Not just a 2X but *10X*. I'd never climbed Mount Everest. I'd never swam the English Channel. Nah, not me. I like climbing and swimming, but at my core I'm a runner. What about running across the Lower 48 States? Nah, Forrest Gump already topped that, and I'd need a full two months off work. Not likely.

What else am I good at? Traveling, flying around the world, hmmmm, *around the world.* I had thought many times about running a marathon on each continent. Just not all in a row. And then it hit me, Six continents, Six Marathons, Six Days! WOW! That would be wicked cool.

My phone beeped, a message from work, a customer needed attention. The dream put away for a moment, but not for too long. The weeks went by and my normal challenges and adventures were being lived out, but in the back of my mind was that crazy, improbable dream.

I had to play with it a bit more, so I started checking in with a few of my "crazy" buddies around the world. What do you think about this idea? Six Continents. Instead of shock and disbelief, their responses were more like, "Now that would be amazing" and "Would you really do that"? To a person, my friends all told me to count them in. They all wanted to be part of the journey. That, my friends, is the benefit of surrounding yourself with a strong and like-minded THPL community.

After several of these exploratory conversations I decided to really see if I could plan this thing out. The mere logistics were the first hurdle I had to cross. An around-the-world plane ticket. What countries? Could I actually make connections in time to get from one place to another and keep the schedule? How much support would I need in each location? Next came the physical challenges: how much training would be required, what would it take to pull this off? I spent the next three months thinking, testing, trying, designing, re-doing, sharing and more. And as each week passed I felt the reality of the improbable becoming possible.

More than a Run

Inspiration and possibility can come from many different sources. For many years the spirit of possibility in my life has been most evident in my interactions with kids, especially High Schoolers. To me, they represent the ultimate in potential. As yet untarnished by many of life's disappointments, they bring unbridled enthusiasm to life. As such, they represent the spirit of possibility for our future, a bright future in my eyes.

As President of the online school Penn Foster, I was fortunate to be able to shepherd a diverse group of high schoolers, helping them to realize the many ways education could change their lives. These students came to know that with the right foundation they could do more, and that with a supportive community around them, obstacles could be overcome and their potential realized. From this most gratifying experience, I saw that mentoring, encouragement, advice and counsel were the secret ingredients that engaged students the best, putting them into the best possible position to succeed.

Fast forward a few years, and with a lifetime of experiences that I'm eager to share with others, I found an opportunity to engage again with the world's future leaders. This time as a Director for ChimeIn.org (The Change Is Me International), an international consortium of Young People (16-24 years-old). CHIMEIN is a "for *purpose*-not-profit" organization, focused on youth empowerment. I was absolutely amazed at the natural way in which these "Youth Ambassadors" embraced life and opportunity, and they served as a powerful inspiration for my 6-Continent Challenge, also sharing in the event by supporting the run and the overall experience.

To take my passion for empowering young people to another level, I connected with the New Roads School in Santa Monica, which was to be the "finish line" for my sixth and final marathon (on *this* leg of the journey that is). I chose New Roads because of what I discovered there, which convinced me that they had to become a part of our CHIMEIN community: an inspired college preparatory program from which an authentically diverse student population, mirroring the rich diversity of Los Angeles, developed a personal dedication to learning, a respect for independent thinking, and an expanding curiosity about the world and its people.

It also struck me as poetic that "New Roads" would be my metaphorical final destination throughout the run. During those long hours on foot and in the air, my mind often drifted to that symbolic moment when I would cross mile 157 (and quite an emotional moment it was!). The "end" of this chapter of my THPL Journey would be the beginning of my "New Road" ahead.

With these important connections made, the run completed, and the proof that the mantra of Dream it, Plan it, Practice it, Do it, really does works, I became more inspired than ever to take (my version) of THPL to the next level.

My Dream took its full form on November 15, 2016, that defining moment when I booked the first flight from Los Angeles to Sydney Australia, the starting point of the challenge. The first day to run was pegged as April 10th. That was still five months away, but I knew the time would fly by, and there was a lot to do.

First I needed to finish my sixth Ironman on November 20th. Then I turned my total focus to running, and a weekly process began taking form. Lots of running, about 95 miles per week, coordination and refinement of the plan, making connections with young and old people in each country to whom I could turn for support.

With six weeks to go, the countdown clock really began steadily clicking in my head. I was feeling great, everything was lining up. I had a great marathon training run in late January with a long run, before and after, building my confidence in the fact that my body was ready. I met with my support team in Las Vegas in February, crossing the "T's" and dotting the "I's" one by one. Every run, every day, was purposeful and focused on the goal. It would be here before I knew it.

With three weeks to go, the planning got even more literal: backpacks, food, clothing, sneakers and a hundred other minute details became the proper distraction to allow for a moment of peace on the way to one of the most amazing moments I had ever contemplated.

Each location started coming to life as local coordinators put in huge efforts to help me plan routes, to organize logistics, to get our youth ambassadors and school partners lined up. We planned as much as we could, we got ready for all issues that we could anticipate, weather, travel, etc. All that was left to do was to get to April 10th.

Countdown Begins – Sydney (1/6)

April 9th, Sydney Australia, and a send-off dinner from our local support crew. Twenty friends were there to cheer me on. It was an amazing evening, sharing the emotions of the moment, the excitement for what was to be, and the knowledge that the world is truly full of really great people, and I was about to meet even more of them. What I came to find came true even before the first step was taken. Beautiful, loving, caring people helping each other sharing in a unique moment. Humbling to say the least.

April 10th, 8:30 am, Sydney Harbor Bridge. A countdown, 10,9,8,7, 6,5,4,3,2,1...and the Challenge started with one step of thousands to come. A stunning visual setting going over the bridge seeing the iconic Sydney Opera House in the distance. My heart raced as my Australian point person leaned over and said, "Be careful with your emotions this week. They could get away from you." What an understatement!

Singapore (2/6)

There are times when we travel that it can all become a blur and hard to get a feel for the location. This was not the case in Singapore. I knew I was in Southeast Asia from the moment I stepped outside the airport. In the early morning hours I ran by group after group of Tai Chi enthusiasts practicing their art in the shadow of the trees lining Singapore Bay. As the run progressed, it was clear I was near the equator (just one degree, a scant 85 miles north actually). Both the heat (90°) and humidity (90%/80° dew point) were as ever-present as they were punishing. Despite the uncomfortable conditions, the city was clean and gleaming, a true "past meets present" experience that helped take my mind off of the fact that I was running through this oppressive, near-liquid atmosphere. This, my second out of six marathons, was to be a simple run, out and back, or so it seemed. Singapore, however, laid down the gauntlet, with its heat index in the danger zone and a taste of struggle from the first step.

Johannesburg (3/6)

There are locations in the world that will spend a lifetime distancing themselves from their past. And as you visit "Joburg" you get the strong feeling that the struggle continues. Hope springs up all around, as big as one could imagine, and yet, there is a sense that there is still so much to be done. My message of possibility and promise was welcomed by a community of amazing people who I learned want to look forward to chase tomorrow with me. Their smiles and warm welcomes were larger than life, their sense of shared purpose undeniable. I will remember the people and this place forever, because on this day, they became a part of me.

London (4/6)

The Queen's palace at Windsor was a fitting backdrop, as the gentle hills and a cool breeze gave the proper feeling to a spring run in the UK. With an enthusiastic support team and peanut butter and jelly sandwiches waiting for me at the end, I set out and kept a strong pace. I amped it up in the last three miles ensuring another sub-four-hour run. I was kind of amazed. I should be *slowing down* at this point in the challenge, and here I was *speeding up*! I was getting *stronger* as the week went on, not more fatigued! My bike escort made navigation easy and fun and with a few local lads joining me at mile 21, the day turned out perfect. Over 100 miles run. Four marathons completed with *only* two to go. Sao Paulo here we come!

Sao Paulo (5/6)

There is a vibe to South America that you feel in your core from the moment you leave the jet bridge. There is a totally unique energetic intensity in the way that you are greeted and the passionate way people behave toward one other. Even though Sao Paulo is one of the most populated (hence congested) cities in the world, April 14th was the *perfect* day to run. The streets were virtually empty because of the Good Friday holiday. A sizeable team congregated for an early morning start from the city center, and over the next 3.46 hours we ran from city street to city park and did it again and again, and with every passing hour, the vibe became evermore friendly and festive. Finishing in Sao Paulo's "central park" at Ibirapuera was an exciting way to end the fifth marathon. By the way, this was the fastest run of the week! Amazing! Woo Hooo!

Los Angeles (6/6)

After more than a week of literal "globe-trotting," it was a sweet homecoming to pass through Border Control at LAX airport. Legs hurt but not too much. I knew, that with just one more marathon to run, I could normalize my discomfort and push through it, especially with the intense energy that I felt pulsing through my entire being. This week, so long in preparation, had literally flown by, and here I was riding the short trip from LAX down the coast to the Redondo Beach pier, an iconic Southern California location, with the Pacific waves crashing on the beach, and blue skies overhead. The route took me north along the beach, hugging the coast toward a spectacular finish. After the passionate intensity of Sao Paulo, the laid-back SoCal energy was just what I needed, through Marina Del Rey, Venice, and then Santa Monica, the run was ready to cross the finish line at New Roads School. A perfect end to an amazing adventure. Yea Baby! It worked! Great to be home! What's next?

Warming Down

Yes, this was invigorating, inspiring, and mind-blowingly fun on so many levels. In the spirit of full disclosure, as expected, there were dozens of stressful moments, miscommunications, and blood sugar lapses, near plane misses, one bloody blister, and one twisted ankle. Yes, sitting on the middle aisle on a 13 hour plane ride was excruciating, not to mention the sleep deprivation that made me feel delirious half the time.

In spite of all that, my mantras kept me going: "Just put one foot in front of the other," "Keep going, don't stop." "Pain is temporary, quitting is forever." Instead of running from the pain, I became curious about it, and I knew that the world was watching the little dot on the Garmin app, so I couldn't stop.

And then there were the *people*. Once again, they gave me proof positive of my profound belief that the world is literally teeming with truly great people who are willing and eager to break out of the past and run toward tomorrow with the best possible convictions of goodness for all mankind. They kept me going when little else could.

In the final analysis, I got to practice what I preach on a higher level than ever before. I had Dreamed It, Planned It, Practiced It and I'd gotten to pass that on to everyone I met.

And in spite of the challenges, <u>I Did It!</u>
I proved that <u>we can do more than we think we can</u>.

I do crazy things sometimes, but I'd like to think that I'm not crazy. I do sensational things sometimes, but I'm absolutely sure that I am no one special. I'm no different than you. We are all both ordinary, and extraordinary.

Here's to the extraordinary you…and The High Performance Life you now get to live.

I have been living this THPL journey for almost twenty years, and each time I stepped into the "Dream it, Plan it, Practice it, Do it," way of life I took the first step knowing the path would be magical. And it happened again. Magic is my new normal…a *mysterious, exciting* and *joyous* normal.

So what is *your* Dream? Are you ready for that next magic experience? What are you waiting for? Give yourself permission right now to go out and find it!

I'll be at your side…here's to the next Dream!

P.S.

How long will we be on our THPL journey? It's a good question. Is it just for a part of our lives? Is THPL only for the best, the smartest, the fastest, the youngest? Do we hit a point when it is no longer necessary to stay on the journey? Should we plan for a different stage later?

The answer is quite simple. Our THPL journey is for *everyone*, every age, every capability, every motivation, every difference, at every moment. It is to be lived for our whole life, not just a a chapter of it. The idea of living The High Performance Life is about each of us, living every day, to get the most that we can out of our lives. It is for us to tap into our potential, to make a difference, to be a role model, to get more than we ever thought we could, by doing more than we think we can at ever point along the way. And it is a lasting journey because it scales to who we are and the stage of life that we are in. We can have resets, we can start again, we can engage and embrace differently as we see fitting to our own lives.

And when we live this way, we really start to feel and understand our purpose, we see what personal fulfillment can be like, and we connect better with the community we live in, our families, our friends, everyone.

When we embrace The High Performance Life journey, we are implored to keep going for as long as we are to be here on Mother Earth, and from this choice we will feel a sense of peace, a sense of harmony, and a sense of balance. It makes this life we have into what it should be: remarkable, meaningful and most of all, *ours*.

Loving life when I just keep going and going!

Ciao,
Joe

Author Bio: Joe Gagnon

(Creator/Founder of The High Performance Life)

Joe Gagnon is an entrepreneur, innovator and transformation executive who has held the role of Partner, CEO, COO and President in a variety of corporations where he has been able to bring together elements of THPL and business for a truly fulfilled life.

Joe is the founder of THPL, The High Performance Life, an avid blogger and serious endurance athlete having completed six Ironman triathlons, ten ultra-marathons, and twenty-six marathons. He has visited all 50 states, logged 4+million air miles, 125,000 miles running and cycling, and spent time in more than 40 countries. His blog The High Performance Life brings together elements of Life, Learning and Fitness for personal fulfillment and improved performance. You can read his daily entries at **http://thehighperformancelife.net.** Or on Facebook at The High Performance Life.

Made in the USA
San Bernardino, CA
02 March 2018